Revised & Updated

The
Survival Guide
for Parents of Gifted Kids

How to Understand,
Live With, and
Stick Up for
Your Gifted
Child

Revised & Updated Edition

The Survival Guide

for Parents of Gifted Kids

How to Understand,
Live With, and
Stick Up for
Your Gifted
Child

by Sally Yahnke Walker

Edited by Caryn Pernu

free spirit
PUBLiSHiNG®

Helping kids
help themselves™
since 1983

Library of Congress Cataloging-in-Publication Data
Walker, Sally Yahnke, 1942–
   The survival guide for parents of gifted kids : how to understand, live with, and stick up for your gifted child / Sally Yahnke Walker.—Rev. and updated ed.
  p. cm.
Includes bibliographical references and index.
   ISBN 1-57542-111-9
   1. Gifted children—United States. 2. Gifted children—Education—United States. 3. Parent and child—United States. I. Title.

HQ773.5 .W35 2002
  649'.155—dc21

                        2002001160

"A Do-It-Yourself Inventory" on pages 26–27 is adapted from VanTassel-Baska and Strykowski, *An Identification Resource Guide on the Gifted and Talented,* Northwestern University, 1988. "How Kids Feel About Being Called Gifted" on page 32 is quoted from Judy Galbraith and Jim Delisle, *The Gifted Kids' Survival Guide: A Teen Handbook* (Minneapolis: Free Spirit Publishing, 1996); and James Delisle, *Gifted Kids Speak Out* (Minneapolis: Free Spirit Publishing, 1987). The young gifted girl on page 97 is quoted from *Gifted Kids Speak Out,* p. 54. The characteristics of gifted teachers listed on page 114 are adapted from *Gifted Kids Speak Out,* p. 80. Material quoted in "Bored No More" on page 115 is from Judy Galbraith, "The Eight Great Gripes of Gifted Kids: Responding to Special Needs," *Roeper Review* 8:1, 1985, p. 15.

Printed in the United States of America
14 13 12 11 10 9 8 7

Free Spirit Publishing Inc.
217 Fifth Avenue North, Suite 200
Minneapolis, MN 55401-1299
(612) 338-2068
help4kids@freespirit.com
www.freespirit.com

Dedication

To my mother,
who has always encouraged me
to be all that I could be, and more.

Acknowledgments

Thanks to Bob, for your support, and to Beth, Sarah, and Amy for teaching me more than I could have taught you. Thank you to all the parents, educators, and students who have touched my life for your ideas and inspiration. Also, thanks to the Free Spirit staff for all your assistance and support.

Contents

Introduction

1. Does your child constantly drive you crazy with questions?

2. Does your child remember things that you would prefer to forget?

3. Does your child like to be challenged with new ideas?

4. Does your child have a vocabulary larger than he is?

5. Is your child aware of situations and question things that are difficult, if not impossible, to answer?

7. Does your child prefer the company of adults or older children rather than age peers?

8. Does your child have a zany sense of humor?

9. Does your child like to take control and organize tasks, seek to tell you and others how to get the task done?

10. Does your child push her limits, refuse to take no for an answer, and act like a junior lawyer at age four?

11. Does your child have a wide range of interests or one consuming area of interest?

If you answered yes to the majority of these questions then *The Survival Guide for Parents of Gifted Kids* is for you. It's for parents whose child has taken them into areas that they didn't know existed or who has shown exceptional talent and intelligence compared to other kids the same age. Your child might or might not have been tested and identified as gifted. Perhaps your child has not been formally identified, but you know that she is different from other children her age. You know that your child is not ordinary. He pushes the envelope, marches to the beat of a different drummer, and makes your job of parenting tougher than usual. If you question what you are doing and why you are so exhausted, proud, and exhilarated, then this is the book for you.

No one ever said it would be easy to raise a gifted child, but no one ever told you it would be this hard. This parenting business can be overwhelming!

You may find that you stand alone in making some of the hard decisions about your child. Large, close families with relatives nearby are a thing of the past, and even when grandparents or other relatives are able and willing to help, they don't always understand what you're going through with your child. Their suggestions just don't work—you've tried them! Your child is different: perhaps more intense, more extreme, more intelligent, and more persevering. *Nobody* seems to understand. That's when this book can help. Think of it as your portable support service, available to answer your questions and give you a pat on the back when you need it.

For more than a decade, *The Survival Guide for Parents of Gifted Kids* has offered help to parents who are faced with the overwhelming task of understanding and nurturing their gifted kids. In this book, you'll learn about the background and history of gifted education, look at what characteristics make these children unique, and discover what needs they may have. You'll learn about the different ways in which schools try to accommodate the special needs of gifted kids. You'll read about traits that may lead to trouble, and what you can do to help.

In this book, you'll find out:

- What characteristics do gifted children share?

- How are children identified?

- How can my child seem to be gifted in one school setting and not in another?

- What are the warning signs of trouble I can watch for?

- What types of programs are available for gifted students?

- How can I advocate for my child?

You can make a big difference in your child's education, and you can help other gifted children by learning how to stand up and be an advocate for gifted education. This gives you helpful pointers on how to work with the system and get things done.

Supporting your child is what parenting is all about. Getting involved is part of raising a gifted child. You'll benefit, as will your child.

The Eight Great Gripes of Parents with Gifted Kids

1. No one explains what having a gifted child is all about.

2. I don't like having my child labeled.

3. Relatives, other parents, and teachers don't recognize that we have unique problems. They assume it's a snap to raise a gifted child.

4. All parents like to think their kids are extra special. Some people think we're on an ego trip, or just plain pushy.

5. The school assumes that "the cream always rises to the top," or that gifted kids will make it on their own, so special programs for the gifted aren't needed. If that's true, then why is my child bored and unhappy with the school?

6. Other people expect my child to be gifted in everything, or to act like an adult.

7. Parents get no support for this challenging job. Once you give birth, you're supposed to know it all.

8. It's exhausting to raise a gifted child! I wish there were ways to make it easier.

Chapter 1
Gifted: Then and Now

*What's in a name? That which we call a rose
by any other name would smell as sweet.*
—William Shakespeare

Has giftedness always been valued?
Do gifted kids today get the education they need?

One way to gain perspective on the role of gifted education in today's
society is to examine its history. By understanding how giftedness has
been recognized and appreciated in the past—and the forces that have
led society to occasionally ignore it—we can better chart a course to
serve the gifted students of today.

One of the first advocates for identifying gifted children was Plato,
Aristotle's teacher and the founder of the first university in around 380
B.C. Unlike other schools at the time, Plato's Academy charged no fees
and accepted girls as well as boys for instruction. Admission was based
on the child's intelligence and physical stamina rather than on the era's
common standard, a family's social position.

Plato advocated testing all children in early childhood. His position
went against the popular belief that giftedness was inherited—a belief
that has surfaced often since then. Now we call this controversy nature
vs. nurture (or heredity vs. environment).

China, beginning with the Tang Dynasty in 618, specifically sought
out gifted children to be sent to the imperial court, where their gifts
could be cultivated. The belief was that the abilities of even the most
gifted children would not develop without special instruction and training, that education should be available to gifted children of all social
classes, and that children should be educated differently according to
their abilities.

In Europe, one of the first efforts to educate promising children
found among the commoners came in 800, when the emperor

4

Charlemagne urged the state to finance their education. During this period in European history, few people outside of the nobility received any schooling whatsoever, and what education and learning were available were dominated by religious fanaticism. Classical learning was relegated to the monasteries in Christian nations, while the Arabs maintained interest in pure science and continued to make strides in astronomy and mathematics. Mosque schools during this period were attended freely by students whether rich or poor, male or female.

The Renaissance era, which dawned in Europe during the late 1200s and lasted through the Reformation of the 1500s, saw a renewed interest in art, literature, and the classical cultures of ancient Greece and Rome. Books became more readily available after the invention of printing and education revived as well.

As Europeans settled in North America, they brought their educational traditions with them. By the time of the American Revolution, however, Thomas Jefferson urged that youth with potential should be provided with a university education at public expense.

The English scientist Sir Francis Galton was one of the first researchers to study intelligence and intelligence testing. Tying into his cousin Charles Darwin's theory of evolution, Galton believed that heredity, through natural selection, was the prime determinant of intellectual ability. In his book, *Hereditary Genius* (1869), he observed that people of accomplishment tended to come from generations of distinguished families, overlooking the fact that children of privileged families are helped in their accomplishments by having greater wealth, education, and opportunity. Today we know that although giftedness appears to have an inherited component, it cannot be accurately predicted on the basis of heredity alone. Two genius parents may produce a child with an average IQ, while parents of limited ability may have a child who is intellectually extraordinary. A child's environment also plays an important role that is still not fully understood.

Until the mid-1800s, when public education was systematized in the United States, education was largely reserved for people who could afford tutors or private schools or people who had connections.

Only in the early 1900s did the American and European public became interested in adapting education to students who had greater- or less-than-average intellectual ability. At that time, the French government commissioned psychologist Alfred Binet, who had developed a test to measure people's "judgment" or "mental age," to identify children who weren't likely to benefit from the general education curriculum and needed special classes.

Binet's work remains one of the most important contributions to educational psychology, although his articles and speeches would still be considered radical today. Binet believed that intelligence is educable—that it can be learned, expanded, and improved.

In 1916, American psychologist Lewis Terman took Binet's test to Stanford University in California, translated it to English, and standardized it for American schoolchildren. Terman's version of the test became known as the Stanford-Binet Intelligence Scale. Ironically, the Stanford-Binet assumes that intelligence is *fixed*—that it *can't* be learned, expanded, or improved. (Your child may have taken the current version of the Stanford-Binet IQ test at one time or another.)

Terman used the standardized test to identify gifted children for a study he was conducting. During the 1920s, he identified more than fifteen hundred children with IQs of 140 or higher. In the general public, the average IQ is 100; Terman's subjects averaged 150. He followed these children from kindergarten through high school and into their thirties, gathering information on their physical, psychological, social, and professional development. In fact, participants in Terman's study who are still alive continue to participate in the ongoing longitudinal research conducted by Terman's successors.

Terman was the first to use the term *gifted,* and his study is the most comprehensive long-term study of people with high IQ ever conducted. He published his findings in a five-volume work, *Genetic Studies of Genius,* which many people consider a classic.

Myths About Giftedness

Terman's study dispelled many myths about giftedness, which until then had made it seem undesirable—a problem instead of a benefit. Today we still hear half-truths and fears about giftedness, remnants of those early myths.

Since ancient times genius has been associated with a troubled mind, and researchers for hundreds of years have tried to associate giftedness with mental and emotional problems. Italian sociologist and criminologist Cesare Lombroso sought out people who had gone insane or committed suicide and linked them to genius in his book, *Insanity of*

Genius, published in 1895. Terman, however, found just the opposite. His data indicated that gifted people are *more* stable than the general population. The instability they may experience, he claimed, stems from their environment, not their giftedness.

More evidence for Terman's viewpoint has accumulated. Psychologists continue to research whether very creative people suffer more often than the general public from certain psychiatric disorders. While a number of studies have found that a higher-than-average proportion of well-known poets, novelists, and artists have been victims of depression and other mood disorders, these findings must be viewed in context. Most creative people with mood problems tend to have relatively mild cases, not serious mental illness. Perhaps the simple fact of being an unusually creative person in our society—a society that doesn't always value such characteristics—contributes to psychological problems. Peter Oswald, a San Francisco psychiatrist and author of *The Inner Voices of a Musical Genius* (about nineteenth-century composer Robert Schumann), believes there is a close relationship between the difficult lifestyle of talented and creative people and their anger, frustration, and depression.

Another myth about giftedness was the "early ripe, early rot" theory, which suggested that gifted people burned out at an early age. Some people thought that children were born with a specific amount of talent, and once they used it up, it was gone for good. If you believed that, you certainly wouldn't want a precocious child. Nor would you dare to encourage early learning. Terman found that no such burnout occurred. He even suggested that children could increase their abilities throughout their lives.

Terman found that gifted people were highly productive, well rounded, well liked, and often chosen as leaders. He also debunked the myth that smart people are necessarily scrawny, bespectacled weaklings (as they are still so often portrayed). Instead, they are usually healthy and well-developed physically.

Although Terman's study is the largest done on giftedness, it's not without flaws. Terman studied predominantly middle-class white children from California and included a disproportionately high number of Jewish children and a disproportionately low number of African-American, Hispanic, and Asian children. He also failed to take into account the influence of socioeconomics on personality differences.

Modern Misconceptions

Misconceptions about gifted kids are still abundant today, which is probably why some parents are reluctant to have their children labeled gifted. (Find out more about the pros and cons of labeling on pages 30–33.) Here are some of the modern fallacies about what being gifted means:

- Gifted children won't know they're different unless someone tells them.

- They'll make it on their own, without any special help.

- They've got everything going for them.

- They should be disciplined more severely than other kids when they err because they should know better.

- They need to be kept constantly busy and challenged or they'll get lazy.

- They should be valued for their giftedness above all else.

- They don't need to abide by the usual regulations, and they shouldn't be held to normal standards of politeness.

- They should be equally mature academically, physically, socially, and emotionally.

The Not-So-Pretty Truth About Gifted Education

Gifted education in the United States has been beset by conflicting public opinion. On one hand, we as a society believe that all children should be allowed and encouraged to reach their full individual potential. On the other hand, we believe that we're all created equal, which means that singling out any group represents *un*equal treatment. But as Thomas Jefferson so eloquently stated, "Nothing is more unequal than equal treatment of unequal people."

In 1941, Paul Witty of Northwestern University conducted a study for the U.S. Office of Education on programs for the gifted. His discoveries made dismal reading. Witty found that only 2 to 4 percent of school districts nationwide had special services for gifted and talented children. When he focused on schools and school systems that did have gifted programs, he learned that those programs that had administrators who supported gifted services were frequently victims of their own success. The good administrators tended to move on to further their own careers, and when they did, their districts often lost their gifted programs.

In 1954, a group of parents and educators in Ohio, who believed that public schools must meet the educational and counseling needs of gifted and talented students, formed the National Association for Gifted Children. The grassroots organization grew rapidly.

The American public at large was motivated to improve education for the nation's brightest students when the Soviet Union launched *Sputnik* in 1957. Dismayed by this 184-pound ball, we blamed our education system for its failure to keep up with the Soviets in math and science. Congress passed the National Defense Education Act of 1958, which for the first time funded testing programs to identify the most able students, as well as guidance programs to encourage these students to attend college, particularly in math and science.

President Kennedy showed a commitment to reaching new heights (educationally and otherwise) when he promised to put a person on the moon. Children were regarded as a natural resource to be developed and used to advance the country and democracy. As a nation, we searched for students with potential, refined and packaged their gifts, and sold their intelligence to the highest bidder—the most prestigious companies.

By the 1960s, as the United States became the clear leader in the race to space, public interest in the special needs of the gifted declined. Social attitudes began changing from a focus on enlisting gifted students to serve the national interest to encouraging all students toward individual growth and developing their full potential. Many people came to believe that using an IQ test to identify gifted students promoted elitism because of biases inherent in the tests. In an era of social protest, protesters everywhere sought to get rid of undemocratic "special treatment."

The Marland Report

Renewed interest in addressing the needs of gifted students emerged in the 1970s when parent advocates for children with special learning needs lobbied state and federal governments and brought suit in court to ensure that public schools provided appropriate education for their children. "Individualized education" became a new catch phrase.

Early drafts of the legislation for these "exceptional" students with special needs included gifted and talented students as one of the categories of students to be served. That language was removed from the bill before it passed, but Congress called on the commissioner of education to study the current extent of programs for gifted and talented students. With this information, educators could evaluate how existing federal programs could be used more effectively and what new programs could be recommended to meet shortages.

The commissioner's report, known as the Marland Report, stimulated interest not only in gifted and talented kids, but also in early education and treatment for students with disabilities.

Here are some of the facts from the Marland Report, which the U.S. Office of Education presented in 1972:

- Approximately 1.5 to 2.5 million children in the United States could be identified as gifted and talented.

- Only 4 percent of these children were being served by special programs.

- Ten U.S. states provided funding for special programs.

- No state provided for all of its gifted students. In those states that had special programs, at best only 50 percent of the gifted students were being served.

- Only twelve universities in the country had graduate training programs to prepare teachers of gifted and talented students.

- More than half of the school administrators surveyed reported that they had no gifted students within their district.

- The overwhelming majority of gifted programs were at the high school level.

- School psychologists, more than other school personnel, were hostile toward gifted students.

- Group IQ tests and teacher identification had failed to identify 50 percent of the gifted.

- Available funding from federal sources for programs for the gifted was being used in less than 15 percent of the states.

- Typically, half of the gifted students had taught themselves to read before starting school.

- Approximately 3.4 percent of dropouts in a statewide survey were found to have an IQ of 120 or higher. Twice as many gifted girls as boys were dropouts.

And here's one last disturbing fact the Marland Report divulged: Because the majority of gifted children's school adjustment problems occurred between kindergarten and fourth grade, about half of gifted children became "mental dropouts" at around ten years of age.

In response to the Marland Report, Congress created an Office of the Gifted and Talented in the U.S. Office of Education and awarded funding of $2.56 million in 1974 to support research and development projects for gifted education, as well as small grants to state and local agencies. If the Marland Report was correct in its estimates of the number of gifted students, that windfall amounted to about a dollar per student. By 1981, however, even this modest effort was diluted when the funding for gifted and talented projects was combined with funding for nineteen other projects into a block grant that states could spend as they chose.

In response, during the 1980s, advocacy groups such as the National Association for Gifted Children began promoting gifted education in a grassroots movement. They were helped in 1985 when the Richardson Foundation surveyed schools about their gifted and talent program offerings. Those who responded said they provided a variety of experiences for their gifted students, but few had anything that added up to a substantial program. According to the study, gifted education tended to be fragmented. Even if a gifted class was available at one grade, there might be no gifted classes in the next. Often, teachers taught what they were interested in, not necessarily what the students needed. Gifted education was regarded as an educational elective, for enrichment only, rather than something absolutely necessary—icing on the cake, rather than real substance.

Advocacy efforts on behalf of gifted children bore fruit in 1988 when Congress passed the Jacob Javits Gifted and Talented Students Education Act. This was the first time Congress officially recognized the needs of highly able students and mandated that an office be opened in the Department of Education. The legislation was based on the idea that research was needed to demonstrate how current educational practices affected gifted and talented students.

In 1990, the U.S. Department of Education awarded a $7.5 million grant to the University of Connecticut at Storrs to fund the new National Research Center (NRC) on the Gifted and Talented called for under Javits legislation. The NRC works to develop new methods of identifying and instructing gifted students and to disseminate information to parents, educators, and policymakers.

Another major outcome of the Javits legislation was the federal report *National Excellence: A Case for Developing America's Talent*. This report, the first on a national level in twenty years, was the most sought-after report issued by the Department of Education in 1993. It was an eloquent statement on the need for gifted and talented education and on the sad state of programs for serving these children. The report highlighted the need for the nation to educate the nearly 3 million gifted children to their full potential to enable the country to compete in a global economy. The report noted problems in the way the United States educates its gifted and talented students. For example:

- Compared with top students in other industrialized countries, American students perform poorly on international tests, are offered a less rigorous curriculum, read fewer demanding books, do less homework, and enter the work force or post secondary education less well prepared. . . .

- Not enough American students perform at the highest levels on National Assessment of Educational Progress (NAEP) tests, which provide one of the few indicators available of how well our students achieve.

The message American society often unwittingly sends to students is to aim for academic adequacy, not academic excellence. The report quotes Gregory Anrig, president of the Educational Testing Service, explaining that students are given a mixed message: "In America we often make fun of our brightest students, giving them such derogatory names as nerd, dweeb, or, in a former day, egghead. We have conflicting feelings about people who are smart, and we give conflicting signals to our children about how hard they should work to be smart. As a culture we seem to value beauty and brawn far more than brains."

Peer pressure to avoid academic excellence can be particularly difficult to combat, especially among adolescents from diverse backgrounds. They sometimes link school achievement to majority cultural values and are accused of selling out their cultural heritage in an effort to be accepted by the dominant society.

National Excellence recommended the following strategies in order to improve the education of gifted students:

- Establish challenging curriculum standards.

- Establish high-level learning opportunities.

- Ensure access to early-childhood education.

- Increase opportunities for disadvantaged and minority children.

- Encourage appropriate teacher training and technical assistance.

- Strive to match world performance levels.

States responded to the report with a number of improvements. Schools reported a new emphasis on curriculum compacting, a broadening definition of what it means to be gifted, improved identification of gifted students from diverse families and low socioeconomic status, and an emphasis on professional development and awareness of the need for accountability for gifted education programs.

To read the complete report *National Excellence: A Case for Developing America's Talent* from the Office of Educational Research and Improvement, U.S. Department of Education (1993), go to *www.ed.gov/pubs/DevTalent/toc.html*.

Standards

In recent years, school reform efforts have focused on educational standards and accountability. Businesses are driving reforms to ensure that graduates will have needed skills. Standards describe what we want students to know and be able to do. States have developed tests aligned with their standards to ensure that students will be taught specific knowledge and skills and be assessed on them. In some states, standards are perceived as being the curriculum. They have taken on great importance and dictate what will be taught and when. Individual schools are often evaluated based on how well their students do on the test.

Although standards are commendable in theory, in practice many problems can occur. Because teachers and schools may be rewarded or punished based on how their students perform, some resort to teaching only material that will be covered on the standardized test. This helps students who are struggling to meet the standard, but it leaves others, especially gifted kids, relearning information they've already mastered. In some cases, knowledge and comprehension are the only thinking skills taught, and gifted kids shrug off the test as an unimportant and useless paper-and-pencil instrument.

Doing Away with Tracking

In the 1990s, many schools moved to eliminate tracking, the practice of grouping students by ability for their classes. The fear was that the labels given to young students in the slower tracks would stay with them as they moved from grade to grade and students may be assigned to a slower track because of teacher expectations rather than because of demonstrated ability and interest. In rigid tracking systems, many argue, students on the lower tracks have lower expectations of themselves, and their teachers likewise have lower expectations for them. As a result, these students receive an inferior education.

The alternative, however, has been a "one size fits all" approach to education, which has its own problems. Trying to teach the same lesson to a mixed-abilities class at the same time can be extremely difficult. Some students learn the material and skills as the teacher intended, some already know it and zone out or distract others, and some don't yet have the basic conceptual knowledge or skills it takes to complete the lesson.

Remember, educational fairness does not mean that all students need to be on the same page on the same day. To support this premise, the movement toward differentiation began to grow from its roots in gifted education. (See pages 104–107, Chapter 5, for more on differentiated curriculum.) Rather than rigid tracking, differentiation calls for flexible grouping based on student readiness, interests, and learning styles to meet the different needs of different students.

The National Association for Gifted Children has developed Gifted Program Standards that provide a blueprint to encourage and guide schools in developing and evaluating high-quality programming. (For more on standards for gifted programming, see pages 19–20.)

We cannot assume that gifted students will have their needs met. It is up to all of us to become advocates for stronger mandates and larger budgets for gifted education services to:

- conduct staff development

- identify students who need a different curriculum

- develop appropriate curriculum and assessments

- evaluate the effectiveness of the programs

Learn More About It

The National Research Center on the Gifted and Talented Newsletter
The University of Connecticut
2131 Hillside Road, Unit 3007
Storrs, CT 06269-3007
www.gifted.uconn.edu/nrcgt/newslttr.html
Explores the latest in research on gifted education issues.

The State of the States Gifted and Talented Education Report by The Council of State Directors of Programs for the Gifted (Washington, DC: National Association for Gifted Children, 2001). Details state-by-state information on gifted education.

The State of State Standards 2000 edited by Chester E. Finn Jr. and Michael J. Pertrilli (Washington, DC: The Thomas B. Fordham Foundation, 2000). This report reviews state educational standards in English, history, math, and science.

Chapter 2
Discovering Giftedness

There is no limit to intelligence . . . or to ignorance.
—Anonymous

What does *gifted* mean?
How can I tell if my child is gifted or talented?
How does my child's school decide who is gifted or talented?
Why do some gifted kids "slip through the cracks" of the system?

One reason it's so hard to decide who's gifted is that the word *gifted* means different things to different people. Here's a look at how some experts, past and present, have defined it:

- Lewis Terman, the researcher known as the father of gifted education, defined gifted as "the top one percent level in general intelligence ability as measured by the Stanford-Binet Intelligence Scale or a comparable instrument."

- Paul Witty, former professor at the University of Chicago, believed a broader definition of gifted was needed to identify students with a high potential for creative expression: "There are children whose outstanding potentialities in art, in writing or in social leadership can be recognized largely by their performance. Hence, we have recommended that the definition of giftedness be expanded and that we consider any child gifted, whose performance in a potentially valuable line of human activity, is consistently remarkable."

- J.P. Guilford, theorist and author of *The Nature of Human Intelligence,* gave the 1950 keynote address to the American Psychological Association convention, which opened the door to identifying and nurturing creativity. He focused on the *nature* of intelligence, rather than on the level. He said that intelligence has three facets or dimensions: content or information, mental operations, and products. He considered people who possess a greater number of abilities in general or a greater number of abilities from a particular cluster to be gifted.

- Joseph Renzulli, director of the National Research Center on the Gifted and Talented, defined giftedness as "an interaction among three basic clusters of human traits—these clusters being above-average general abilities, high levels of task commitment, and high levels of creativity." He is critical of giftedness being identified as a high IQ score.

- John C. Gowan placed the gifted child movement within a humanistic psychology framework: *"Gifted* means having the potential to be verbally creative, while *talented* means having the potential to be non-verbally creative."

- The Marland Report, which led to federal funding for gifted education stated, "Gifted and talented children are those identified by professionally qualified persons who by virtue of outstanding abilities are capable of high performance. These are children who require differentiated educational programs and/or services beyond those normally provided by the regular school program in order to realize areas of their contribution to self and society."

- Howard Gardner, a Harvard professor who developed a theory of multiple intelligences, identified eight types:

   1. *Linguistic:* often thinks in words, likes to read and write, learns best by verbalizing or hearing and seeing words.

   2. *Musical:* likes to sing or hum along to music, appreciates music, may play a musical instrument, remembers melodies.

   3. *Logical-Mathematical:* thinks conceptually, manipulates the environment in a controlled and orderly way, likes logic puzzles and strategy games, enjoys computers.

   4. *Spatial:* thinks in images, likes drawing and designing things, enjoys construction toys, is fascinated with machines.

   5. *Bodily-Kinesthetic:* has athletic or dance talent, may be good at typing, sewing, carving, or other activities that require fine motor skills.

6. *Interpersonal:* understands people, shows leadership, success-fully mediates when people have conflicts.

7. *Intrapersonal:* shows deep awareness of his or her own feel-ings, dreams, and ideas; studies independently; may be nonconformist.

8. *Naturalist:* is sensitive to environmental surroundings, includ-ing nature, and observant of how systems work.

- The Columbus Group—a group of psychologists, educators, and parents led by clinical psychologist Linda Silverman—recognized the central role atypical development plays in the lives of gifted children: "Giftedness is asynchronous development in which advanced cognitive abilities and heightened intensity combine to create inner experiences and awareness that are qualitatively dif-ferent from the norm. This asynchrony increases with higher intellectual capacity. The uniqueness of the gifted renders them particularly vulnerable and requires modifications in parenting, teaching and counseling in order for them to develop optimally."

- Françoys Gagné, researcher at the University of Quebec, defined giftedness as having outstanding natural potential in at least one ability domain. He said that *talent,* or outstanding performance, is developed through systematic training and practice. One can be intellectually gifted yet not academically talented, according to Gagné, due to underachievement.

- The U.S. Department of Education issued *National Excellence: A Case for Developing America's Talent* in 1993, which defined gifted as follows: "Children and youth with outstanding talent perform or show the potential for performing at remarkably high levels of accomplishment when compared with others of their age, expe-rience, or environment. These children and youth exhibit high performance capability in intellectual, creative or artistic areas, possess an unusual leadership capacity, or excel in specific aca-demic fields. They require services or activities not ordinarily provided by the schools. Outstanding talents are present in chil-dren and youth from all cultural groups, across all economic strata, and in all areas of human endeavor."

- Writer and researcher Stephanie Tolan defined giftedness in terms of asynchronous development. She stressed that giftedness is an internal reality, mental processing that is outside of norms. Achievement, in contrast, is merely an expression of that mental processing. Achievement may fluctuate depending on a student's immediate situation but giftedness does not.

- Robert Sternberg, a professor at Yale University, argued that giftedness comprises five elements:

  1. *Excellence:* the gifted are superior in some dimension or set of dimensions relative to their peers.

  2. *Rarity:* gifted people possess a high level of an attribute that is rare relative to their peers.

  3. *Productivity:* the dimension(s) in which a gifted individual shows excellence leads to productivity.

  4. *Demonstrability:* the dimension(s) that determine giftedness must be demonstrated through one or more valid assessments.

  5. *Value:* the society must value the superior performance in the demonstrated dimension(s).

How Schools Identify Gifted Kids

It's tough, if not impossible, to identify every potentially gifted or talented student, especially when schools have limited funds and personnel. Schools attempt to identify students who need a *different* educational program based their readiness, passion or interests, and learning style or learning preference. Most schools have a screening and selection process to avoid arbitrarily assigning students to special programs.

According to the National Association for Gifted Children, a school's process for identifying which students qualify for gifted programs should contain these important elements:

- a comprehensive and coordinated effort to determine eligibility

- assessment instruments that measure diverse abilities, talents, strengths, and needs

- a profile of each student's strengths and needs to help in planning appropriate intervention

- identification procedures and instruments based on current theory and research

- written policies that include procedures for informed consent of parents, student retention in the program, reassessment of students, exiting the program, and appeals processes. .

In general, schools screen children for gifted programs using one or more of the methods described in this section. The purpose of screening should be to cast a wide net so that as many students with potential as possible can be considered. There are many screening mechanisms (self-nomination, parent recommendation, class performance, portfolios, grades, etc.), but most districts use IQ tests, achievement tests, and teacher nominations. Schools may use one or a combination of these methods, but they generally aim for quick and cost-effective methods. Because of what we now know about the brain and how people learn, fewer and fewer schools rely on one test score alone. The more information a school has on a child, the better able they are to program for the child's needs.

Some schools initially administer a test to all students for a first screen of the entire student population. Students who are identified as potentially gifted by their test score may then go through a series of tests, data collection efforts, or reviews to assess who would benefit most from services. Many schools use a matrix to generate a composite score for individual students. This method looks at the range of assessment instruments given to the total population and then weighs the scores according to predetermined criteria. Weighted scores are plugged into the matrix for each student, and the scores are ranked. The top students are selected for the program. The district sets the cutoff at a designated percentage to meet the state or district criteria.

The difficulty with a matrix is that because it looks only at scores rather than individual students, the learning needs of some students may go unrecognized. Given that this method of selecting students often has strict cutoff points, a child could be in a gifted program or receive services one year and not the next, depending on who else is in the pool. Another danger is that schools using this method may exclude a student who is superior in one specific area but not on a wide range of assessments.

Who is identified as gifted depends on how giftedness is defined. For example, if the school believes that gifted means having an IQ of 130 or higher, then an IQ test will be used to identify students and those scoring 130 or higher will be provided services. If, on the other hand, the school is looking for demonstrated high performance, then a portfolio of student artwork, evidence of achievement in math, or demonstrated leadership may be examined. Above all, the identification process a school uses needs to be tied closely to the program and curriculum model it implements.

Should students be identified to fit the program that exists or should students be identified for their promise and abilities and the program tailored to meet their needs? Usually, schools identify gifted students who fit the existing program, because that is cost effective. In an ideal setting, however, schools have a responsibility to educate students to their potential, which often necessitates special programming.

In any case, the identification process for gifted programming should be a matter of public record, and you need to know what process your child's school employs. The school's gifted program coordinator should be knowledgeable about the process and able to explain it to you. If your district does not have a gifted program coordinator, then the principal, curriculum coordinator, or an administrator in charge of special programming should be able to help you.

Some schools have an appeals procedure for students missed in the selection process. Other districts require additional testing, documentation of performance, or additional references, which may be the parent's responsibility or expense.

Along with clear identification and selection procedures, school districts should also have a written exit procedure that gives clear guidelines for students leaving the gifted program. If a program is not an appropriate match for the student, exiting the program may be necessary, and you need to understand why and how that will happen.

Standardized Tests

Standardized tests have uniform procedures for administering and scoring the test, and they have established norms that allow one individual's score to be accurately compared to those of others who take the test. Standardized tests must also demonstrate validity (that they actually measure what they are intended to measure) and reliability (that one person taking the test is likely to achieve the same score over several administrations of the test, with multiple raters, and with different test questions). In other words, a standardized test should show how one ranks compared with others, measure what it is supposed to, and produce the same results if given time and time again.

Group Intelligence Tests

Group intelligence tests—the IQ tests administered by schools to a large group of children—have certain drawbacks as screening tools for gifted programs. Their best use is to help identify those students who need subsequent identification with more accurate individual measures. Although they're commonly used for initial screening, they often miss many gifted students, notably smart kids who have trouble reading, kids who have emotional or motivational problems, kids who come from poor homes, kids from culturally diverse backgrounds, or kids who are just learning English. And the younger the child, the less accurate the group test results tend to be. Since there is so much more to any child than his or her IQ, as many as half of the potentially qualified children may miss being identified in this way. Also, a child's IQ score may vary from one test to another. Schools shouldn't rely on this often-inaccurate test as their only screening method, yet many do. Some districts use an IQ of 125 as a cutoff point to determine who gets into their gifted program, while others might set the cutoff at 140. Some families whose children score just below the cutoff opt to have them retested using an individual IQ test.

Although there are no standard IQ levels for intellectual giftedness, the following guidelines have been suggested by the newsletter of the Hollingworth Center for Highly Gifted Children (Fall 1994):

Mildly gifted IQ range: 115 to 129
Moderately gifted IQ range: 130 to 144
Highly gifted IQ range: 145 to 159
Exceptionally gifted IQ range: 160+

Individual Intelligence Tests

Individual intelligence tests are more accurate than group tests when it comes to predicting intelligence, but they're also costly and time consuming. Some schools may provide them on request, but many parents find that if they want an individual test, they have to have it done independently.

Even though individual tests are more accurate than group tests, they likewise shouldn't be the only criterion for admitting a child to a gifted program. Many experts say that these tests don't test intelligence; instead, they test academic aptitude within a specific culture. Intelligence tests also do a poor job of measuring creativity, and they often do not discriminate well between moderately, highly, and exceptionally gifted children. If a test has a low ceiling, it may not show intellectual differences among the students who achieve the top scores. For example, a student who is highly gifted and a student who is mildly gifted may both achieve the top score on a test if the scale does not go high enough for the highly gifted student to demonstrate what she knows and can do. When these gifted kids are tested on instruments with higher ceilings or tests used for older students, they have the chance to show what they actually know because the test has a broader range of scores. Consequently, some researchers continue to use a test known as the Stanford-Binet: L–M because it is the only test that identifies subgroups of gifted children, including the highly and the exceptionally gifted.

Buros Institute of Mental Measurements
University of Nebraska-Lincoln
21 Teachers College Hall
Lincoln, NE 68588-0348
(402) 472-6203
www.unl.edu/buros
This site provides comprehensive information on standardized tests, including online links to descriptions and reviews of more than 10,000 published tests and research instruments, including intelligence tests.

Standard Achievement Tests

Achievement tests measure what students have learned rather than attempt to gauge their potential. Most schools administer achievement tests at regular intervals, and the results are readily available. Like the results of group intelligence tests, the results of achievement tests should be regarded with caution when schools identify children for gifted education programs. Student proficiency in a particular area may be reflected on an achievement test, but these tests are not designed to measure giftedness. Not all gifted kids score well on standardized achievement tests.

On achievement tests, the grade-equivalent score does not indicate the grade level at which the gifted child has the capacity or potential to successfully function; rather, it indicates the average sore earned by students at that grade level. Some bright kids don't do well on achievement tests because they consider them unimportant and race through them to finish. Other bright students may not have been exposed to the material covered by the test. Achievement tests typically have low ceiling scores, which means that gifted children may score at the top of the range, so parents and teachers have no way of knowing what the child really knows and can do. In other words, it prevents gifted students from showing their true potential. In these cases, children need to be tested at a higher level. Sometimes it's a good idea to test bright children with older kids or those who are a grade or two ahead. These off-level tests give gifted young people a better chance to show what they know.

Achievement Tests

- **California Achievement Test** gives twelve scores: reading (vocabulary, comprehension, total), mathematics (concepts, comprehension, problems, total), and language (usage, mechanics, structure, spelling, total).

- **Iowa Tests of Basic Skills** assesses fundamental skills for grades 1–12. Scores are expressed as grade equivalents, percentile norms for special groups, and age equivalents.

- **Metropolitan Achievement Tests** contain traditional, norm-referenced tests and criterion-referenced data for

continued

students in grades K–12. Scores are provided for reading, mathematics, language, social studies, science, and writing.

- **Sequential Test of Education Progress** measures English expression, reading, mechanics of writing (spelling, capitalization, punctuation), mathematics, science, and social studies for grades 4–6, 7–9, 10–12, 13–14.

- **SRA Achievement Series** measures skills in reading, mathematics, language arts, reference materials, social studies, and science. Two forms are available at each level.

- **Stanford Achievement Test** measures language skills, reading comprehension, mathematics skills, science, social studies, and auditory skills. Five levels arc available for grades K–12.

Teacher Nomination

When identifying kids for participation in gifted programs, some schools skip tests and rely on teachers' recommendations. Other schools use tests in conjunction with teacher recommendations.

Teachers can provide valuable insights if they are trained to look for the true characteristics of gifted and talented children. But the recommendations of untrained teachers aren't always reliable. Some classroom teachers tend to identify only those students who achieve well, turn in homework on time and neatly done, and otherwise do what's expected of them. It's easy for a busy teacher to overlook students who are highly creative, messy, unambitious, or divergent thinkers. It is also easy to miss children who come from diverse backgrounds or who are just learning English.

Teacher insights should be part of, not all of, the identification process. As with standardized tests, up to half of the qualified kids may be missed when the teacher's opinion is the only identifier. Researcher Jon Jacobs found that kindergarten teachers nominated gifted kids with only 4.3 percent accuracy. Parents do a much better job than teachers in identifying their children as gifted. Parents nominated fewer total children and were more accurate in their nominations. Teachers need training to understand the characteristics of gifted students before they can reliably identify them.

One mother who felt sure that her second-grade son was gifted asked to have him tested. The teacher said she'd do it, but she hadn't noticed anything unusual about the boy. "The only problem is that he reads his reading book when we're supposed to be doing math," the teacher said. Tests later confirmed that the boy was, in fact, gifted.

Parent Nomination

As a parent, you can provide wonderful insights into your child's abilities, and some schools give you the opportunity to provide input.

A Do-It-Yourself Inventory

Here's a checklist you can use to determine whether your child might be gifted or talented. (You might use the results to support your case with your child's teacher.)

What special talents or skills does your child have? Give examples of behavior illustrating these talents or skills.

_____

_____

_____

_____

_____

Read each item and decide how well it describes your child.

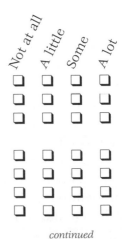

	Not at all	A little	Some	A lot
1. Is alert beyond his or her years	❏	❏	❏	❏
2. Has a high activity level	❏	❏	❏	❏
3. Shares the interests of older children or adults in games and reading	❏	❏	❏	❏
4. Sticks to a project once it is started	❏	❏	❏	❏
5. Is observant	❏	❏	❏	❏
6. Has an extraordinary memory	❏	❏	❏	❏
7. Uses many different ways of solving problems	❏	❏	❏	❏

continued

	Not at all	A little	Some	A lot
8. Is aware of problems others often do not see	❏	❏	❏	❏
9. Uses unusual ways of solving problems	❏	❏	❏	❏
10. Wants to know how and why	❏	❏	❏	❏
11. Likes to pretend and has a vivid imagination	❏	❏	❏	❏
12. Has an excellent sense of humor	❏	❏	❏	❏
13. Asks a lot of questions about a variety of subjects	❏	❏	❏	❏
14. Is not necessarily concerned with details	❏	❏	❏	❏
15. Is sensitive and compassionate; responds intensely to noise, pain, frustration	❏	❏	❏	❏
16. Plans and organizes activities	❏	❏	❏	❏
17. Has above average coordination and ability in organized games	❏	❏	❏	❏
18. Progresses through developmental milestones at an advanced rate	❏	❏	❏	❏
19. Enjoys her or his own company	❏	❏	❏	❏
20. Makes up stories and has unique ideas	❏	❏	❏	❏
21. Has a wide range of interests	❏	❏	❏	❏
22. Gets other children to do what he or she wants	❏	❏	❏	❏
23. Demonstrates highly developed language skills	❏	❏	❏	❏
24. Enjoys and seeks others with similar interests	❏	❏	❏	❏
25. Is able and willing to work with others	❏	❏	❏	❏
26. Sets high standards for herself or himself	❏	❏	❏	❏
27. Chooses difficult problems over simple ones	❏	❏	❏	❏
28. Is fascinated with books	❏	❏	❏	❏
29. Likes to do many things and participates whole-heartedly	❏	❏	❏	❏
30. Likes to make his or her ideas known	❏	❏	❏	❏

Creativity Tests

Creativity tests ask students to solve problems creatively, and their answers are scored for fluency (the number of responses), flexibility (the ability to change one's mindset), originality (how unusual the responses are), and elaboration (the amount of detail included in the responses). These tests show promise in identifying divergent thinkers—children who come up with many different responses to a problem—who may be overlooked on IQ tests.

Here's a roundup of what creative gifted children are like. (Some of these traits are described in more detail in Chapter 3, pages 45–64.)

1. Show intense curiosity about many things and constantly ask questions about anything and everything.

2. Come up with a large number of ideas or solutions to problems and questions, often offering unusual, off-the-wall, or clever responses.

3. Are uninhibited about expressing themselves and disagreeing with others, including adults; they don't easily give up strongly held opinions.

4. Take risks and may be adventurous and speculative.

5. Are intellectually playful. They fantasize, imagine ("I wonder what would happen if . . . "), and fool around with ideas, changing and adding to them. They like to adapt and improve institutions and things.

6. Have a keen sense of humor and see humor where others don't.

7. Are unusually aware of their impulses, show emotional sensitivity, and seem to be open to the irrational in themselves. Boys may show a freer expression of interests generally considered more feminine, while girls may possess a greater than usual amount of independence.

8. Are sensitive to beauty and notice the aesthetic side of things more than the average child does.

9. Don't necessarily conform to the usual. They may be comfortable with disorder and do not mind being different.

10. May be good at giving helpful criticism and won't accept what you or their teachers say without examining these ideas or rules critically.

Portfolios

Collections of a student's work show what the student can accomplish. Portfolios can demonstrate growth over time and showcase examples of your child's best work. They can include photographs, videos, or audio-tapes to demonstrate performance in areas not measured by paper and pencil instruments, including the visual and performing arts. Be sure that the material you include is dated and that entries have notations as to why you chose them. Include any expert evaluations and reviews of your child's work.

Zach's test scores were below the cutoff for entry into his school's gifted program. His mom knew that his ability far surpassed his age peers and therefore asked for a meeting with the gifted program coordinator and teacher. She had put together a portfolio, a collection of his work, since he was two years old. In this collection, she noted that he started reading at age three and she kept a bibliography of books he had read, all dated. She had a videotape of Zach reading at different ages. She noted his interests and had pictures of projects he completed, along with pictures he'd drawn and explanations of them. It was work well beyond his age peers. His case was reconsidered, and he was admitted to the gifted program based on his portfolio.

Top Percentile of Honor Roll

Identifying gifted kids by their grades alone tends to favor students who strive to achieve by traditional measures. A student's position on the honor roll often depends on the classroom he or she happens to end up in, and it can vary greatly from building to building and from district to district. Besides, some hard-working students will always manage to get excellent grades without being unusually intelligent or able.

Pupil Motivation

Task commitment—or stick-to-it-iveness—often leads to great accomplishments. Dr. Joseph Renzulli, discussing Terman's studies of the gifted, noted: "The four traits on which the most and least successful groups differed most widely were persistence in the accomplishment of ends, integration toward goals, self-confidence and freedom from inferiority feelings. In the total picture, the greatest contrast was in all-around emotional and social adjustment and in drive to achieve." The problem is that measuring motivation is difficult.

Peer Nomination

Students themselves often have a fairly good idea of who the gifted kids are in their class, but identification of gifted students can't become a popularity contest. With younger children, some testers use cartoons to locate those students who are known by their peers for their cleverness, leadership ability, or ingenuity. In one test, the test-giver shows a child a picture and asks, "Who would Moppet ask for help when he is lost? Or when he's in need of a special invention?"

What Happens Next?

If you suspect that your child is gifted or talented, the next move is yours. Talk to your child's teacher, and, if necessary, discuss your observations with the gifted program coordinator or principal.

Be sure to keep records of your child's progress and achievements so you can back up your claims. You may even want to keep a portfolio or notebook with examples of your child's work, a list of books read, and pictures of projects. Remember to date them. In some cases, a gifted child's ability is evident, especially in the performing arts or athletics. In other cases, special gifts or talents are less obvious and harder to see.

In some instances, school personnel may be the first to spot a child's talents, but *you usually know your own child best*. In fact, if a teacher is *not* trained to identify giftedness, the bright, creative child may appear to be more of a pain than a pleasure in the classroom. If your child fits this picture, you may need to speak with the school counselor, psychologist, administrator, or curriculum specialist. (For tips on getting your school to improve its gifted programming, see Chapter 6.)

The Question of Labels

Some parents, as well as a number of experts, question the value of labeling a child gifted. But labels already exist, and yes, they create expectations. When you ask children, they already know quite accurately who's in which readiness group. Kids are very aware of which students already know the information or can learn it faster and more easily. Even if we adults don't acknowledge that some children are smarter than others in specific areas, our kids will.

Ability tracking and special programs for the gifted do not fit well with the current educational focus on cooperative learning and classroom inclusion. *Tracking*—putting kids in ability-based groups—is controversial for valid reasons. Many educators have a real concern for kids who are labeled (sometimes inaccurately) and never given a chance to rise above that label. The goal should not be to label the student, but rather to identify the student's learning needs. But once teachers identify a student's need for a different curriculum, they have a problem that didn't exist before. Now parents may ask if the school is doing everything possible to stimulate their child. It feels like a bigger responsibility than before.

For gifted children, knowing that they are in the advanced or high track may only reinforce something they already knew about themselves. Acknowledging giftedness doesn't necessarily make kids conceited, which some people are afraid of. Many gifted kids have described finding social comfort, peer acceptance, and self-acceptance when they are placed in programs that include other gifted children.

In fact, being with peers of similar ability can be a humbling experience. The elitist attitude originates when the gifted student is the only one in class who gets the correct answer or is always the one who offers it first. Knowing that other kids have similar response times can be a real growth experience.

How Kids Feel About Being Called Gifted

- "I don't mind being called gifted as long as I'm not stereotyped as being perfect."

- "Sometimes people get the wrong idea when we are labeled as gifted. It doesn't mean being better than others. It means I learn differently and faster than the others in my class."

- "I feel comfortable with the label if I'm in a group of people who are considered gifted—then I want to be considered gifted, too. But I'd certainly never introduce myself as a 'gifted person.' I'd never seek out that label, but I'd always want people to say, 'Yeah, she's a bright student, she's an inquisitive student, she's going to go far.' I think the label has positive and negative connotations."

- "I do not like being called gifted; it's embarrassing and it's like bragging."

- "I don't know of any other word to replace gifted but I wish someone would think of something."

Labels can cause problems if you're not careful. According to research conducted by Dewey G. Cornell, a clinical psychologist and professor at the University of Virginia, it's better for parents not to emphasize the gifted label. Cornell found that those children whose parents openly refer to them as gifted have less favorable self-images, are more prone to anxiety, stress, and depression, are less well-liked by their peer groups, and have more behavior problems.

According to Cornell, these difficulties are due to parents focusing too much on this one aspect of their children's personalities and having too many expectations. When parents do this, kids are likely to think their self-worth depends only on being gifted.

Cornell's advice is to downplay the label and encourage your kids to be well-rounded, kind, helpful, and friendly. In his study, the children of parents who did this had fewer problems than the others.

How Parents Feel About the Label Gifted

- "I'm not certain that the gifted label is in the kids' best interests, or in the parents'. To me, it fosters inflated egos and sometimes elitist attitudes, and may increase the pressure to excel to justify their giftedness."

- "Those who don't have a child in the program have a problem with the label. I don't."

- "For my child, who's very hard on herself, thinking she's gifted makes her feel better about herself. However, it's embarrassing at times."

- "I think it causes resentment from their peers. There must be a better term to use."

- "There's more of a chance the teacher will be interested in the children and able to develop challenging activities."

Kids Who Fall Through the Cracks

Some gifted kids fall through the cracks of the system when their teachers miss the signs of their talent. If your child fits one of the categories in this section, her abilities may not show on standardized tests. Giftedness is not always obvious. You'll need to pay close attention to see that your child's needs are met in the classroom. All children have a right to learn new information and to learn how to struggle with difficult tasks. When gifted kids don't get the attention they need, they may underachieve, disrupt the class—even fail. According to Barbara Clark, author of *Growing Up Gifted,* gifted children need to be engaged in learning that challenges them and enhances their talent at their level of development or they will regress.

Start recording some of the activities your child has been involved in, and what she was aiming at by doing them. (If you don't know, ask her.) Is she pursuing a special interest? Do her abilities surprise you? Present this information to the gifted program coordinator or to your child's teacher or principal.

Kids with a Lot of Energy

High energy mixed with low tolerance for frustration and pressure can signal trouble. Many little boys are very tactile learners who don't easily sit still and do the paper and pencil tasks teachers require. That can make it difficult to identify their intelligence, and even tougher for teachers to meet their needs. In the classroom, gifted kids are sometimes thought to have an attention deficit hyperactivity disorder (ADHD), while out of the school setting their giftedness may show up better.

The difference between active giftedness and ADHD can be difficult to sort out because the characteristics may be similar. Here are a few questions you can ask in looking at your child:

- **Do the behaviors occur at only a certain time of day? Or only during certain activities? Or in certain environments? Or with only certain people?** Gifted children typically do not exhibit problem behavior in all situations. To one teacher, they may appear to have ADHD, but not to another. They may appear to have behavioral problems in their regular class, but not in music or at Scouts. Children with ADHD, on the other hand, more typically show their problem behaviors in all settings, but they may occur more frequently or strongly in one setting than another.

- **Is the student able to concentrate when the activity is interesting to him?** Gifted children sometimes do not pay attention in class. The inability to focus may be related to boredom, mismatched learning style, or curriculum.

- **Have any curriculum modifications been made to try to correct the inappropriate behaviors?** Gifted students usually maintain consistent efforts and high performance in classes when they like the teacher or the content and are challenged. Some gifted students become intensely focused to produce a product that meets their incredibly high, self-imposed criteria. This does not happen for children with ADHD.

- **Could the inappropriate behaviors be due to inappropriate placement, insufficient challenge, or lack of intellectual peers?** When the gifted child learns more easily and more quickly than her age peers, she may spend more than half her class time waiting for the others to catch up. Her response to unchallenging, slow-moving lessons may be misbehavior or inattention.

- **What is the child's perception of the problem behavior?** Gifted students may have difficulties following rules and regulations. They may question, engage in power struggles, or become angry at a system that is not meeting their needs.

- **Does the student feel out of control? Do parents feel that the child is out of control?** The gifted child's activity is usually directed toward specific goals or occurs episodically. Children with ADHD exhibit problem behaviors more continuously.

Determining whether a child is gifted, has ADHD, or combines both giftedness and ADHD can be extremely difficult and requires a comprehensive individual evaluation. It is best to have one professional who attains rapport with the child administer many evaluation instruments—including intelligence, achievement, and personality tests—and consider parent and teacher rating scales and observational data. Portions of some tests may determine if your child has a learning disability. Personality tests may show an emotional problem (for example, depression, anxiety) that is causing behavior problems. Evaluation needs to be followed up with appropriate curricular and instructional changes. This may mean adapting lessons to allow for prior knowledge or a different learning style.

Don't be afraid to bring up the fact that your child could be gifted. Many professionals have not had training or experience in gifted education. You may hold the key to the correct diagnosis.

Gifted Girls

How are gifted girls different from girls in general? All girls need love and support for their freedom and development. Gifted girls, however, require support that is sensitive to the fact that their giftedness is not necessarily valued in society. Girls and women who have high abilities may be seen as aggressive, unfeminine, pushy, or impolite for showing the same behaviors that are rewarded in boys and men. Unfortunately, not only does sex-role stereotyping still exist, but it becomes increasingly evident in the middle and high school years. Some girls struggle to hide their excellence when the person they want to date is struggling with schoolwork. Parents, more than anyone else, can influence their daughters by providing opportunities for their talents to develop. Expectations, opportunities, and cultural values can deeply influence whether girls with exceptional talents will use and develop them.

Gifted girls need help if they perceive a discrepancy between their ability and self-image. They may achieve well but discount their accomplishments. On the other hand, they may perform poorly, even with high ability, and blame their poor performance on low ability. Some adapt by becoming uninterested in school and excelling socially, showing leadership in positive or negative ways. All of these behaviors signal a need for help.

Parents and teachers can help a gifted girl in these ways:

- Listen to her. Help her to recognize and accept her giftedness.

- Help her find friends who value her abilities and are not threatened by them.

- Help her find role models. Read biographies of gifted women. Look for women who make a difference in her community.

- Avoid sex-role stereotypes. Let her play with cars and blocks if she wants to.

- Encourage activity. Don't overprotect her.

- Allow her to make mistakes and even fail. Be there when she does to help her through the hard times.

- Encourage her interest in science and math, as well as in more traditionally feminine fields.

- Discuss gender stereotypes that you encounter in advertising, on TV, in the movies, on rock videos, or in literature.

- Assign household chores on a nonsexist basis. Both girls and boys can cook, do laundry, and wash the car.

- Encourage her to spend time with her father, her grandfather, or another male relative or friend, doing something that they both enjoy, even if it's a typically masculine activity.

- Let her know you value her abilities. Let her fall in love with something and pursue it.

Kids with Disabilities

Thomas Edison, Helen Keller, and many others all possessed special gifts, along with disabilities. Consider Edison's mother. She didn't give up on her son, even when his school did. She homeschooled Thomas and even set up a place for him to carry out his experiments in his father's barn. Like her, you can become an advocate for your child.

Students who are "twice exceptional" possess an outstanding gift or talent and are capable of high performance, but they also have a disability that makes some aspect of academic achievement difficult. Some of these students may have their needs identified and served, but most fall through the cracks of the system, especially students with learning disabilities or learning differences (LD).

Many twice-exceptional children are not failing enough to be referred for testing services. This creates a big problem. They are often told that they are lazy or forgetful, or that they aren't trying hard enough. Gifted children with LD need to be identified and helped early. This often calls for specially designed tests that compare them with other disabled kids. With the results of these tests, the school can work together with you and other resource personnel to design programming that meets these kids' needs. These children need strategies such as tutoring, consistent programming, peer group support, mentorships, integrated studies, individualized attention, and kind words. They crave honest, positive comments and encouragement, not nagging. The focus needs to be on what they can do, rather than on what they can't do.

There are at least three categories of children who are gifted and LD and go unrecognized.

The first group includes students who have been identified as gifted yet have a hard time in school. These students are often believed to be underachievers. Their underachievement may be blamed on poor self-concept, lack of motivation, or even laziness. Their LD usually remains unrecognized. As school becomes harder and harder, their academic difficulties may increase to the point where they are falling behind peers to such a degree that someone finally suspects a disability or they are no longer regarded as gifted.

The second group includes gifted students whose giftedness goes totally unrecognized. The learning challenges are severe enough that they have been identified as having LD. This group of students may be larger than many people realize. A study conducted at the University of Connecticut–Storrs found that as many as 33 percent of students identified as having LD had superior intellectual ability. Their disabilities led to depressed IQ scores or poor assessments, grossly underestimating their intellectual abilities. Their potential remains unrecognized and so it never becomes a cause for concern or the focus of their instructional program. They rarely if ever receive the gifted services they need.

The largest group of unserved gifted students with LD are those whose abilities and disabilities mask each other. These children receive neither gifted nor LD services. Because they work at grade level, they are thought to have average ability. They are not believed to have special problems or to have special needs. Sadly, however, they perform well below their potential. A learning disability may be suspected in later years when work becomes more demanding. The help they needed to accommodate their limitations has not been available, so their academic problems increase. Seldom is their true potential ever recognized.

It is difficult, if not impossible, to label all of the characteristics that define the population of gifted students with LD; however, there are some clues that should be considered in identifying these students:

- evidence of an outstanding talent or ability

- evidence of a discrepancy between expected and actual achievement

- evidence of a processing deficit

Teaching Strategies and Techniques

Regardless of the program model or the setting, academically talented students with LD require a curriculum geared to their strengths rather than their weaknesses, as well as a variety of strategies, adaptations, and accommodations to help them succeed. Teachers can help by making tasks meaningful, cutting big tasks into smaller units, and using relevant praise, peer tutoring, and cooperative activities. Successful adults with disabilities can be role models, helping students develop aspirations and self-esteem. Special educational accommodations, such as technology, can help academically talented students overcome their LD and move ahead in their area of strength. A word-processing program for students who have difficulty with writing or spelling can help them get their ideas down. For children who have difficulty with computation but wonderful mathematical problem-solving abilities, a calculator may be the key to success. Peer tutors, untimed tests, and tape recorders may all help the child who finds the regular assignment impossible. These children need to be exposed to new topics and develop techniques that help them learn about their own thinking and processing of information.

A complete assessment battery is needed to identify and plan interventions for gifted students with learning differences, including an individual intelligence test, an achievement battery, indicators of cognitive processing, and behavioral observations.

Look for the following problems, which could be getting in the way of identifying your child as gifted or talented:

- difficulty with memorizing, learning math facts, spelling, reading, timed achievement tests, or remembering instructions with more than two steps

- a wide gap between subtest scores (great in verbal, awful in math), gaps in scores between different tests (high today, low tomorrow), or a profound difference between behavior at home and at school

- poor motor coordination

- repeated ear infections, especially within the first three years, since these can cause problems with a child's hearing, and learning problems may develop as a result

- difficulty completing easy work, but ease with harder concepts

- poor self-concept; a feeling of being stupid

- allergies

Because there are many different types of gifts and disabilities, gifted students with learning differences represent a diverse group. What they have in common is a discrepancy in their performance.

Children from Diverse Cultures

Children from diverse cultures and those learning English may be over-looked because their home culture or language is different from what the teachers are used to or value. Although they might well be gifted or talented, they don't appear to measure up to the standards of the major-ity culture, and their self-esteem suffers when this happens.

If you suspect this is happening to your child, you can make it a point to get to know the staff at your child's school. Let them know about your family. Tell them about any special family activities your child excels in to keep them informed of your child's achievements or accom-plishments outside of school.

Sara, a young girl from a Spanish-speaking family, had a high IQ, but since English was her second language, her teacher didn't have any idea how bright she was. By the time Sara was in second grade, she had memorized many Bible verses and performed a major role in a church-sponsored play. Her teacher didn't know anything about these activities until Sara's mother brought them to her attention.

Teachers need to put aside the question of verbal skills, at least for the time being, when they're looking at someone from a home where English is not the main language. Teachers can identify giftedness no matter what language students speak if students:

- act independently

- know how to get their ideas across, including nonverbally

- show leadership and initiative

- are imaginative

- approach problems flexibly

- show signs of being able to think abstractly

- learn quickly

- remember and use information and ideas well

- show unusual curiosity

Young Children

Because tests don't accurately measure what young children know, this population is often overlooked. The problem is further complicated by the fact that specialists in gifted education are not usually specialists in early childhood education, and vice versa. Few states provide funding for programs designed for young gifted children.

Still, the sooner gifted kids are identified and given appropriate challenges, the better their chances of reaching their full potential. Too often, young children who are taught without special curriculum differentiation learn to adapt to the average classroom expectations and never reach beyond them. This frequently happens before third grade, which is when most schools begin the identification process for gifted programming.

Children from Low-Income Homes

Parents with low incomes may be too busy struggling with the tasks of survival to think much about whether their kids are gifted. The effort it takes to get a child into a good gifted program may seem overwhelming when you are struggling to find transportation to work. Here's where connecting with a sharp teacher can save the day. Many successful adults whose families were poor can point to teachers in their past who made a difference by recognizing their abilities and offering special encouragement and opportunities.

Gifted students from low-income homes show superior ability in one or more of the five following areas.

1. **Learning.** They demonstrate verbal proficiency and advanced vocabulary, possess ready information on a variety of topics, have rapid insight into cause-and-effect relationships, catch on quickly, and observe closely.

2. **Motivation.** They show powers of concentration and complex organization. They may be self-critical, assertive, persistent, and motivated by sports, music, and concrete information.

3. **Leadership.** They tend to dominate, take initiative, take on responsibility, be looked upon as leaders, adapt easily to new situations, and enjoy being with others.

4. **Creativity.** They display intellectual playfulness and take risks. They may be known for their sense of humor, curiosity, and the ability to improvise and generate large numbers of ideas. They may be sensitive to color, design, and artistic understanding or have exceptional physical coordination.

5. **Adaptability.** They handle many outside responsibilities while meeting school demands, deal well with problems caused by complex living conditions or limited resources, have mature judgment and reasoning, and transfer learning from one situation to another. They may be knowledgeable about things others remain unaware of.

Kids Who May Get Left Out of Programs

Here are some of the characteristics that can keep gifted kids out of a gifted program when teachers haven't been trained in identifying gifted kids. Sometimes kids are not identified as gifted because they may:

- be bored with routine tasks

- refuse to do rote work or homework

- be self-critical and impatient with failures or mistakes

- have difficulty in getting moving from one topic to the next

- be critical of others, especially authority figures they see as "dumb"

- make jokes or puns at inappropriate times

continued

- disagree vocally with authority figures

- overreact if things go wrong because they are so emotionally sensitive

- have no interest in details, turning in messy papers

- be stubborn, nonconforming

- tend to take over or dominate others

Putting Things in Perspective

In any effort to identify gifted kids and make sure that no one gets overlooked or mislabeled, mistakes are inevitable. It helps to remember that the definitions of gifted and talented change with time and vary by culture. It also helps to remember that school staff really do not identify giftedness; rather, they identify a need and then program for that need.

Once, hunting was a highly prized skill; today, hunting is primarily a sport that some people consider barbaric. Fire-bringers, fortune-tellers, athletes, and entertainers have all been esteemed in certain periods and cultures but not in others.

If today we were to place a premium on IQ and creativity, what might we produce tomorrow? If our society is concerned only with money, sports, and entertainment, what message are we sending to our children? Where are the gifts we seek?

Current research in identifying students for gifted education programs recognizes the different ways in which students display giftedness and calls for more and varied authentic assessments. Instead of relying strictly on intelligence and achievement test scores, multiple criteria need to be used, including nontraditional measures such as observations or portfolios. Many professionals in the field of gifted education believe that these practices will help identify gifted students who better mirror the diversity in our society.

Learn More About It

American Association of University Women Report: How Schools Shortchange Girls by the American Association of University Women Educational Foundation (New York: Marlowe & Company, 1995). A report on gender stereotyping in schools. The executive summary and report are available online at *www.aauw.org/research/girls_edu cation/hssg.cfm.*

Exceptionally Gifted Children by Miraca Gross (New York: Routledge, 1995). A look at exceptional giftedness with stories of real children.

Frames of Mind: The Theory of Multiple Intelligences by Howard Gardner (New York: Basic Books, 1993). An intelligent discussion of the different ways people think and can excel.

Growing Up Gifted: Developing the Potential of Children at Home and at School by Barbara Clark (New York: Prentice Hall, 2001). Packed with detailed information on all aspects of giftedness and gifted education.

In Their Own Way: Discovering and Encouraging Your Child's Multiple Intelligences by Thomas Armstrong (New York: Jeremy P. Tarcher, 2000). A clearly written guide aimed at parents and teachers.

Keys to Parenting the Gifted Child by Sylvia Rimm (Hauppauge, NY: Barrons, 2001). Practical advice on working with schools and managing the problems of parenting gifted children.

LD Online offers many helpful articles on what it means to have LD and be gifted. Visit *www.ldonline.org/ld_indepth/gt_ld/gifted_ld.html.*

Uniquely Gifted: Identifying and Meeting the Needs of the Twice Exceptional edited by Kiesa Kay (Gilsum, NH: Avocus Publishing, 2000). A book on twice-exceptional students that brings together chapters by parents, educators, researchers, and students themselves.

You Know Your Child Is Gifted When . . . A Beginner's Guide to Life on the Bright Side by Judy Galbraith (Minneapolis: Free Spirit Publishing, 2000). A light-hearted introduction to life with a gifted child.

Chapter 3

Living with
Your Gifted Child

*That is what our children can offer us and we can offer them:
a chance to learn from them, even as we try to teach them.*
—Robert Coles

What are gifted and talented kids like?
How can I be a supportive parent to my gifted child?

Every child is a unique individual, but your gifted child shares certain characteristics with other gifted children. Your child may learn differently, act differently, and react differently from most other children who are the same age. You can no doubt think of instances when your youngster has done something especially charming, precocious, or embarrassing. It's likely that you have been impressed or surprised by some unexpected behavior.

This chapter looks at the characteristics most bright youngsters share. With this knowledge, you'll be able to do the best possible job of meeting your own child's special needs. Keep in mind that gifted kids are as different from each other as they are similar. When a child has a disability, we talk about the skill deficits or other areas that require attention. A gifted child has a surplus, however, rather than a void. The gifted child has more! This is what often gets them (and sometimes you) into trouble.

Endless Questions

Gifted kids are hungry for knowledge. They are trying to find information about their world. Some of them want to know all about everything. They can be like grasshoppers, jumping from subject to subject, interest to interest. Other gifted kids want to know about one specific topic at a time. They become the resident experts on that topic.

Their questions are endless. From the minute they wake up until they collapse, their minds are at work, trying to make sense of their world. Even at lights out, their questions continue. You'll notice this even when they're very young. More than one parent has put it this way: "My child is like a sponge, trying to soak up everything."

Kids Ask the Darnedest Things!

- "Where do stars go when they fall?"

- "Why in the United States do we not use all of our farm-land when there are people starving in the world?"

- "Why does snow melt around the base of the tree first and not in other places? Do trees generate heat?"

- "Why hasn't there been a cure for the common cold?"

- "Why do we have wars?"

As you know by now, some of your child's questions *can* be answered (even if not by you), while some don't have definite answers. It's always a relief when a child asks something you or he can look up—except, of course, when the answer is beyond a young child's comprehension. A bright child can ask more questions than a wise parent can answer.

What can you do to prepare for the barrage of *why*s, *when*s, *what for*s, *who*s, and *how come*s? Start early to accumulate a good set of reference books—a current almanac, an atlas, a book of world records, a book of facts, a dictionary, a thesaurus, a one-volume encyclopedia, perhaps even a whole set of encyclopedias. Find appropriate Web sites to explore. You'll want to help satisfy that curiosity as soon as possible, whenever possible, and you can't always get to the library.

As for the tougher questions, be honest. Depending on your child's age, you might say something like, "That's a really good question. A lot of adults have asked that question, too. The problem is, we don't have a great answer to it. What do *you* think? Would you like to know what I think?"

Learning with Activity

Gifted kids and (their parents) soon find out that learning and discovering are intense processes that produce activity. Some children are so active, in fact, that they're misdiagnosed as having attention deficit hyperactivity disorder (ADHD). One important difference is that gifted kids often appear driven to explore their world, to find an answer to their questions. They love complexity. Sometimes they even make things more difficult than they really are. They use their seemingly endless energy to achieve a goal: getting to know the world better. They are active and involved, both mentally and physically. Children with ADHD, in contrast, tend to be active without a particular goal or purpose. (For more on ADHD and giftedness, see pages 34–36.)

Because their minds are as active as their bodies, many bright kids have difficulty going to sleep. They have a hard time settling down and quieting their minds. They may be the first in their age group to give up naps. Plan for lots of active, imaginative, outdoor play to make use of some of that energy.

Don't try to have a stimulating conversation or watch an exciting movie and then plan on having your active gifted child go right to sleep. Downtime is necessary. Relaxing, even predictable, bedtime stories serve a real purpose besides enjoyment—they help kids' minds gear down, as well as their bodies. Listening to soothing music can also help.

Remember When?

Gifted and talented kids generally have excellent memories, which they frequently put to good use by reminding their parents of things they may have forgotten (or wished to forget). One mother reported that she got a speeding ticket when her son was three years old and he *still* remembered it—time, place, and speed—at age nine.

Gifted children recall years later who gave them what at holiday time, and what promises were made and not kept. Do comments like these sound familiar?

- "Three weeks ago last Thursday you promised we'd go to the park playground. We still haven't gone. How come?"

- "Last year in September my teacher said that we would go on a field trip. We never did."

You'll keep your child's trust a lot longer if you don't make promises you aren't sure you can keep.

Early Learners

Young gifted kids may walk and talk earlier than their peers, although there are exceptions. A few very bright, perceptive youngsters wait to talk until they can communicate in complete sentences, or they may wait to walk until they can do so without falling. These children usually learn in one or two repetitions. They hear something once and it's learned, even information you wish they wouldn't hear—let alone use.

Two-year-old Lynn and her mom were visiting one of her mother's friends. Her mom's friend had a collection of bears in her basement. When the friend asked Lynn if she would be afraid to go to the basement, the girl explained that she remembered the bears were not alive from her last visit six months earlier. In the basement, Lynn proceeded to count the bears. One bear, two bears, three bears . . . all the way to thirteen bears. Her mother's friend was amazed.

If your child is like most gifted kids, she probably possesses a motor mouth that rarely shuts down. These kids also tend to have sophisticated vocabularies that sometimes alienate them from their peers who don't understand the big words. For example, a young gifted child may want to discuss dinosaurs with his playmates, but rather than talk in general terms, he'll get specific about brontosaurus, stegosaurus, and tyrannosaurus rex.

Bright children not only hear and understand big words, they can also apply them in the correct context. One three-year-old was fooling around to delay her bedtime. When her mother asked what she was doing, she replied, "I'm procrastinating!"

Asynchronous (Out of Sync) Development

Gifted kids may be one age emotionally, another age physically, and still another age intellectually. Many gifted children have one set of friends who are their age peers and another set of friends who are their intellectual equals.

Bright children need others like them to play with and share ideas. You'll notice that when there are only a few such youngsters in a larger group, they tend to find each other and form strong attachments.

When the other children your child's age are not at his mental level, he may claim that someone much older is his best friend. It's common for a very smart five-year-old to choose a nine-year-old down the street to hang around with, explaining, "He's got good ideas." This turns into a problem when your child's older friend wants to go to the park and your five-year-old isn't allowed to cross the busy street yet. The nine-year-old may take off on a two-wheeled bike and leave your little one behind. This also has implications for the fourth-grader who is best friends with the college sophomore. Both share a love of computers, but the fourth-grader is not interested—and should not be involved—in college activities.

New situations and problems are bound to come up when your child hits the teen years. His intellectual peers are dating, driving, maybe drinking, but he's neither emotionally nor legally ready for those milestones.

Talented children who have skipped a grade, or even multiple grades somewhere along the way, may suffer the most intensely from this discrepancy. Physically they may not be able to keep up in sports. Intellectually they may be advanced. Socially and emotionally they may have peaks and valleys. Gifted kids often feel different to begin with, and adolescence intensifies this feeling, while the desire to be accepted causes even more pressure. Above all, your child needs to feel that you love and understand him.

What are the two most difficult periods of a gifted child's childhood?

1. **The preschool years,** when children don't know exactly what's wrong but somehow know they're different. They may even wrongly see themselves as dumb.

2. **The teen years,** because peer pressure is so great. When bright teens feel the pressure to be like everyone else, they sometimes *under*achieve.

Sometimes problems arise at home because of the gap between a child's intellectual and emotional ages. You may say to your child, "Act your age," when that's exactly what he's doing. Silliness is a prime example. You might scold your gifted child for acting silly, even if you would tolerate the same behavior in another child.

Some adults, even though they believe that kids will be kids, feel that gifted kids should "know better." A five-year-old may be able to read at a fourth-grade level or solve amazing math problems, but he's still only five years old. Accidents may happen, thumbsucking may persist, shoelaces may go untied, and babyish behavior may surface from time to time.

Never punish your child for acting childish because a gifted child should know better. If giftedness is linked to the punishment, the giftedness is almost certain to go underground. Try to relax and let your child be a kid for as long as he needs to be. Take the word of many parents who have gone before you: your silly child will be grown up and out of your hair before you're ready.

Don't you wish, just a little, that you had time for more silliness in your busy life? One gifted high school senior summed it up by saying, "If we don't let kids act like kids when they are younger, then they will play and act like kids when they are older and it may be totally inappropriate."

The Motor Skills Gap

Your young child's manual dexterity is probably not advanced beyond her years, and she may actually lag behind her age mates in this area. This can be frustrating, since her understanding and knowledge go far beyond her ability to work with her hands.

A bright child's handwriting may not be as good as either she or her teachers would like it to be. Gifted kids often find the act of writing slow, tiresome, and discouraging, especially since their minds can work far faster than their pencils. Consider letting your child dictate her ideas into a tape recorder when she's fed up with writing. Take dictation from her and let her illustrate her story. Once they master keyboarding, many kids find computers very freeing, especially for creative work, since they eliminate much of the tedium from correcting errors.

Help your young child develop her small muscles by playing with modeling clay, finger-painting, or stringing beads or cereal. She probably dislikes restrictive, prescribed ways of doing things, so permit her the freedom to express herself with art materials. Teach handwriting as an art form—calligraphy. This makes it fun and challenging to form letters, rather than sheer torture. Physical activity of all kinds helps youngsters become well-rounded in their motor skills.

Coping with Young Lawyers

Have you ever found a person three feet high who could out-argue your best efforts? If your gifted child is like most, he learned early to use his excellent verbal ability to get exactly what he wants. But just because he's good at it, don't let him dictate the rules and regulations of the house. Children feel more secure if their parents set a few important rules and stick to them, no matter what. Giftedness is no excuse for disobedience or obnoxious behavior.

When you deal too strictly with most children, they tend to get angry and act aggressively toward other children. This goes for bright children, too, only they may take this further and may also learn to lie or steal at an early age if they feel they need to. So it's especially important that you treat your child with fairness and respect.

Giftedness doesn't mean moral superiority. That is, your child doesn't deserve more lenient rules just because he's smart. But he may learn more quickly than other children what consequences to expect from what sort of behavior—so he doesn't have to make the same mistakes repeatedly. Maybe. He may also learn the skill of manipulation and use it.

Bright children need to understand the structure of the world so they can function within it. If gifted kids continually manage to outsmart their parents and teachers and gain control, as they attempt to do at times, they may end up feeling lost and confused. Even youngsters who have superior knowledge appreciate the security of knowing that some-one wiser and more experienced is in charge.

As your child matures and you see him making sound decisions, you'll be able to trust him more and more. If he argues with you because he truly believes truth and justice are on his side, at least listen carefully to what he has to say. There's no shame in being won over by the superior arguments of a young lawyer, as long as he's not just arguing for the sake of arguing—and as long as you don't go against what you deeply believe in or know is unsafe.

Sometimes it helps to set boundary rules. Boundary rules are those that are nonnegotiable Although they are firm, they vary depending on the age of the child: no skipping school, no alcohol, curfew on school nights, lights out, no playing with matches, etc.

With practice, you can tell when your child is arguing just for the sake of pushing limits and when he really has rational principles on his side. If he can base his arguments on having proved his responsibility in some area, maybe it's time to loosen the rules and broaden his freedom.

The Company of Adults

Your child may be more comfortable with you and other adults than with other children her own age. This kind of dependency happens for a couple of reasons. Gifted kids often feel the frustration and limitations of their age, and they may, in fact, interact better with adults than with their peers. They may truly enjoy adult conversations and prefer adult company. Your gifted daughter may feel that you are her best friend.

Gifted kids can also usually figure things out quite well, but they may not yet have gained the ability or skills necessary to carry out what they understand intellectually. So they feel that they need adults to help them fulfill their goals.

A five-year-old once asked me to write a letter to the editor of our local newspaper. He was deeply concerned about an injustice, and he knew that those in authority wouldn't listen to a five-year-old but might consider his solution if it were presented by a teacher. I sat down with him and he dictated his ideas to me. I submitted his letter under his name. He was satisfied that his ideas were presented, and I was satisfied that I was assisting him while using his words.

Helping is fine, but don't get caught in the trap of talking for your gifted child—as in, "Mom, I want *you* to tell my teacher that I couldn't do _____." The bright child, who recognizes that a teacher will more readily listen to a parent's ideas and requests, figures, "Why not get Mom or Dad to do the talking?" It's important that your child knows you support her, but she also needs to learn to speak up for herself.

The Importance of Risk-Taking

Some of us are glad that our kids aren't more daring than they are, at least when it comes to physical thrills and spills. But when it's a matter of taking a chance on a new activity or sticking one's neck out to meet an intellectual challenge, it's sad to see some gifted kids hold back and not even try. They tend to be self-critical and see only their inadequacies. These insecure children want to know what something is all about, how it will work, and what's involved *before* making a commitment.

One parent reports, "Our daughter, although bright, can be difficult to motivate. She set standards for herself based on the group of students in her class. Placing her with others that work at her level (and above) motivates her to work harder and come closer to doing the level of work she is capable of."

Some bright kids won't try anything new. They *hate* to be wrong, look foolish, or not know what's happening. They want to observe others in action before trying something new themselves. Watching others is a fine way to learn something—within reason. But if your child's caution is prompted by a strong fear of failure, you'll want to help him feel better about himself. He needs to know that not being able to do something right the first time is *not* the same as failing and that even repeated failures or errors don't make him an inadequate person.

Be sure not to fall into the trap of making killer statements like, "That's ridiculous!" or "That could never work!" Such statements discourage your child from using his imagination—which is the last thing you want to do. Show that you value your child's work, along with the sometimes uneven process he went through to complete it. You can encourage your child by saying, for example, "I can see you really put forth a lot of effort on that." Risk-taking requires an atmosphere of acceptance. Give your child permission to try it and see what happens.

Give yourself permission to learn something new, too—something that involves taking a risk. Model struggle for your child. Too many youngsters think that everything comes easily for adults. Try a new sport, learn a new skill, explore a new art form, learn a new language with your child.

One way to help your youngster abandon the assumption that all questions have only one correct answer is to pose problems that don't have just one answer. Try these:

- How would you improve the house?

- What would you do if you won the lottery?

- Where do you think the ideal place to live would be and why?

- What would an ideal school be like?

So You Have a Comedian

Gifted children often have a mature sense of humor. They have an advanced understanding of the world and are able to capture the subtle humor that they see. They catch the punch lines in jokes—both those they hear and those they make up—when other children may miss the humor completely. Because of this, your child may become frustrated when other kids don't get the joke. Some bright youngsters prefer adult company partly for this reason.

Smart kids often get a special kick out of puns and plays on words. One parent reported that her son appreciated and understood adult jokes from about age four.

Just be warned: If thwarted, the gifted child's keen sense of humor can turn to biting sarcasm. If you see this habit forming, point out that people who always put others down, even jokingly, are not liked.

Gifted Wordplay

- The second grader told his teacher the school was really popular despite not having air-conditioning. When she asked why she was told, "It has a lot of fans."

- While comparing different thermometers for various temperature readings one of the thermometers fell over. Five-year-old Evan joked, "We'd better get our coats because the temperature dropped."

continued

- Five-year-old Tran said to her father, who was leaning over a bowl of spaghetti, "Watch out! If your tie falls in the plate, you'll have Thai food."

- Eight-year-old James told his teacher that the terrorists who attacked New York and Washington, D.C., sure didn't know much about the United States. "The terrorists spell *freedom* FREEDUMB when they think that they can take away our spirit and freedom," he explained.

Fast Learners, Deep Learners

Almost all gifted kids learn basic skills better and faster than other children do. They need fewer repetitions and less practice to master new information. When they have to review over and over again things they already know, they quickly become bored and lose their motivation. The result is careless errors, sloppy papers, or unfinished work. Some teachers perceive this as a lack of motivation and use it against a bright child, saying, "He doesn't deserve to be in the gifted program. He can't even do the regular work in class. He's flunking daily assignments!"

Gifted and talented children often have many interests, but they usually like to concentrate on one specific area at a time. They become "specialists" at an early age as they gather and retain an amazing amount of information about a chosen area.

Take heart, parents: Kids *do* pass from one all-consuming passion to another. But next year could be worse! If you thought dinosaurs were bad, *living* reptiles could follow. One mother finally had to make a rule: Nothing alive, and nothing that had ever *been* alive, could be brought into the house without her permission. Her daughter had been bringing home roadkill to dissect so she could study animals' insides. She was not satisfied with pictures and overlays of the systems of the body. She wanted the real thing.

Most bright children like to initiate projects. They tend to have hobbies and collections. They like to discover knowledge by figuring things out for themselves. At times, they may take on more than they can handle. One middle-school student wanted to study civilizations. He wanted to learn about the world and all its people from the beginning of time.

Daunting task! Breaking it down to a specific time period and a specific culture made the task much more manageable and his energy much more focused. Students who take on too much are doomed to almost certain failure. Many times they don't know how to break the topic into smaller bites. They may need to learn that when one area is accomplished, they can then move on to the next. Approached in this way, a large project becomes more manageable and doable, more likely to breed satisfaction and success.

Help your child be realistic in attacking projects. Often a youngster will do part of the planned work—just enough to satisfy her need for information—and then quit. After all, research can be the most fascinating part of a project; writing it up feels anticlimactic. If your child needs to produce a finished product, you may need to lend a guiding hand. Otherwise, be prepared to accept unfinished projects and frequent shifts in direction. Discuss the change of interest, and then let your child move on without guilt.

You may also need to help your child meet deadlines for school projects. Many bright youngsters wait until the last minute to do anything. Time lines with interim goals help students break the project into bite-sized pieces, so that the entire work is not so overwhelming.

Super Sensitivity

Gifted and talented folks of all ages tend to be acutely aware of problems. With their strong powers of observation and awareness, it's common for them to develop fears and anger about war, starvation, poverty, abuse, violence, and all the other injustices in the world. In other words, they worry about Big Stuff! With their heightened sensitivity to society's hypocrisy and injustice, gifted children may feel despair and cynicism, even at a very young age.

Researchers Jeffrey Derevensky and Elaine Coleman investigated the fears of gifted kids and compared them with those of children of normal intelligence. Among younger gifted children, the most common fears included some form of violence and nuclear war. This emphasis on violence may reflect what kids are reading and hearing about in the news media—reports of kidnappings, terrorism, molestations, murders, and other terrible acts.

Bright children were also found to have a variety of miscellaneous fears, emphasizing their increased awareness of the world. Some of their concerns included death and disease, pregnancy and abortion, unemployment, lack of friends, loneliness, bankruptcy, being abandoned, lack of love, and mental disorders.

Gifted kids are so perceptive that even at a young age they realize the inevitability of death. They question the meaning of death, and some even become obsessed with dying. They may act out dying or bring home dead animals to bury.

While death is a natural process, coping with the death of a family member is not easy. Few of us in this death-denying culture feel comfortable talking to children about death, but children can end up feeling guilty and somehow responsible when everyone's feelings are kept hidden. Their questions need to be answered frankly, in order to avoid the unspoken message that death is so bad that it shouldn't be faced.

The heightened sensitivity of gifted children may lead them to perceive social rejection, even when none is intended. It may also lead them to believe that something is wrong with them. It doesn't help when other children ridicule them for reacting strongly to something trivial.

Intense sensitivity can produce both positive and negative effects, depending on the child's perception and his response to it. Advanced intellectual development makes a child uniquely vulnerable. (For more on heightened sensitivities of gifted kids, see pages 71–76.)

Sound Minds in Sound Bodies

Parents need to be careful not to minimize gifted children's need for lots of physical activity. At times, their bodies are (and should be) as active as their minds. Moving to music, learning to ride a bike, running, and walking are just a few of the choices. Help your child use his imagination to come up with ways to get physical and to have fun at the same time.

Here are a few stimulating physical activities to try:

- Creatively change games to bring new excitement to old favorites. For instance, when playing table tennis, the person who wins the first game plays the next game with her "wrong" hand (left hand if she's a righty).

- Play "All on One Side." This is a volleyball game with four or five players on one side, none on the other, and a balloon for a ball. Each player volleys the balloon to another player, then scoots under the net. The last player to touch the balloon taps it over the net and scoots under. The receiving players try to keep the balloon in play and repeat the process. The object is to get your team to the other side of the net and back as many times as possible.

- Walking is a terrific lifelong exercise. Take different kinds of walks together with your child. For example, try a never-before-seen walk. As you travel a familiar route, look for ten things (or fifty) you've never noticed before.

Intense Concentration and Relaxation

Gifted kids often have a long attention span for things that interest them, but not necessarily for work that is assigned to them. Your youngster may be so totally preoccupied with a book, computer, or project that he won't hear you say it's time for a meal. He's not ignoring you; he's just absorbed and totally unaware.

When your child does not hear you calling, try a gentle hug or touch. Eye contact works wonders. Yelling and nagging are useless. They simply develop children who learn to ignore you and become parent deaf.

You'll reduce everyone's frustration if you let your child in on plans and scheduling ahead of time. You probably wouldn't like it if someone told you, "Put that book down right now! We have to go to the store."

You'd probably prefer to hear, "I need to go to the store at three o'clock. I'll let you know ten minutes before we have to leave." If your child is the kind who becomes very engrossed in and stimulated by a project, you may have to help him learn to wind down.

At times, your child may feel bombarded with sensory information as if everything is converging on her. She'll need to get away, either by relaxing where she is, or by physically escaping to a quieter place. Can you think of a room or a corner in your home where your child can go for some privacy and peace? Gifted children are particularly sensitive to the sights, sounds, and other stimuli of their environment. They may be deeply affected by nature, music, or colors. They notice small nuances in their world that others may be blind to. They need a safe, quiet, peaceful place where they can go to relax and just be by themselves. Some bright children have a hard time getting to sleep. Their minds are on overload. They can't leave a stimulating book or TV show and go straight to bed without something in between. They need time to unwind. Or sometimes they'll go to sleep with no trouble, then wake up in the middle of the night with their heads full of wonderful ideas. A tape recorder beside the bed can give them a way to record their thoughts and release them so they can get back to sleep.

Physical exercise can be very relaxing, but some children get such a high from it that it becomes another habit. One boy became so accustomed to that high, excited feeling that he was almost using it as a drug. For him, exercise was no longer a form of relaxation but another activity he felt driven to do. If you notice your child becoming overinvolved in any activity, step in and help him strike a balance in his life. Encourage him to try new things, to play, to be with friends, and even to take time off just to be lazy. It's okay to relax.

Relaxation Techniques for Kids

- Teach your child a simple method to focus the mind or meditate. For example, you might suggest that she clear her mind, focus entirely within herself, ignore any external distractions, and play calmly with any thoughts that enter her mind.

- Counting breaths can serve a dual purpose: it's relaxing, and it helps to control a wandering mind. Have your child count each breath, one by one, up to ten, then start over again. He can repeat this process as often as necessary to feel calm and refreshed. Explain that if his mind wanders at any time during this exercise, he should go back to one and start counting again.

- Suggest a more physical way for your child to relax. Have her sit in a comfortable position or lie down, close her eyes, and relax. Then ask her to tense all of the muscles in her body at once. Have her clench for a few moments, then relax her muscles all at once, letting every part of her body go limp.

- Another physical relaxation technique involves beginning with one body part (perhaps the fingers of one hand), tensing it and then letting it go limp. Proceed to consciously relax every part of the body, one by one, from the ears down to the toes.

Neatness . . . Not!

It won't surprise you to learn that bright children aren't always neat. In fact, they tend to have a special tolerance for confusion and junk. We're talking about kids who may solve tomorrow's energy crisis but can't find a pencil today because it's buried under open books, half-completed projects, Lego cities, stamp collections, and other evidence of their many and varied interests.

Neat assignment papers are probably not a priority, and a neat room—neat by your standards—is almost always out of the question. Gifted kids in general hate to throw things away. They can tell you exactly when and where they found the pretty rock that's on the desk, and which bird lost the feather that's under the bed. They're so acutely observant and aware of details that they notice if something is missing. Moral: Respect their belongings, and don't expect to get away with simply tossing what *you* are tired of.

Schools don't teach time- and clutter-management skills, so you'll need to come to the rescue with a bit of organizational savvy. For example, you might hold a weekly or monthly "what do I want to keep?" session. Although your child may prefer to hold on to all her school papers, have her sort through them, choose those with special value to her, date them, and put them in a special place or folder.

A variety of storage boxes can work wonders. Have your child label folders by the month and file them in a big box. At the end of the school year, have her sort through them and think, "What do I want to remember about this year?" Those things she wants to save can then go into a portfolio, a special container that holds a collection of work that demonstrates growth over time or examples of best work. Boxes can also be used to classify things your child considers important or pieces of precious artwork. When the boxes are full, then it's time to sort, reorganize, and decide what to toss—or get more boxes.

Allow your child her own designated space, which will undoubtedly be less tidy than you'd like. You may certainly set a few house rules, such as everything has to be off the floor on Saturday mornings (or whenever the vacuuming is done); no food litter allowed in bedrooms; and all personal belongings are to be removed daily (or weekly, if you can stand it) from common areas, such as the living room.

Early Readers

Some gifted kids are self-taught readers. With most of these young children, we don't know when and how they cracked the code. Early reading isn't always a sure sign of giftedness, but it can be a clue.

Some children learn to read as early as age three. Some are taught to read by parents or learn at preschools or daycare. Other bright youngsters have other interests, and reading may not be a priority for them. In fact, the bright child who doesn't read by the end of kindergarten or first grade should not be eliminated from (or passed over for) gifted services. Similarly, the preschool child who reads shouldn't be admitted to a gifted program on that criterion alone.

Studies indicate that early reading (often before the age of four), early and prolific use of language, unusual alertness in infancy, early manipulation of symbols, and early abstract reasoning ability are typical of profoundly gifted children. The average age at which highly gifted children sight-read an easy reader is younger than four, which is also true for profoundly gifted children. This has been found across cultures and languages as well as time periods.

It is not unusual for a highly gifted young child to comprehend such books as *Little House on the Prairie*. This creates a problem in kindergarten or first grade when basic decoding skills are taught and emphasized. Parents and schools need to enrich and accelerate the curriculum to meet the child's advanced needs.

Gifted children master reading, like so many other tasks, when they're ready and when they see the benefits it can bring them. Many seem to begin reading on their own without letting us in on how they do it. Although early reading is common among children with intellectual gifts, some do not read until they are in school. Sometimes they also possess a disability that prevents them from reading early. Giftedness and learning disabilities are not mutually exclusive. (See pages 37–39.)

Communicate, Communicate

Most bright kids are cooperative, sociable, and well liked. They're often regarded as leaders. Parents need to make sure that these talents are channeled in a positive direction. Many gang leaders are kids whose talents have been negatively channeled.

It is a misconception that the more talented the child, the easier it is to parent this child. Quite the opposite is true. Parenting of any extreme of ability requires greater resources of all kinds. It also requires you to communicate, communicate, communicate.

Make it a point to know what your child does after school, in the evenings, and on the weekends. Know who his friends are. Get to know his friends' parents, too. Call and introduce yourself; you may find that they feel the same way you do and are pleased to hear from you. If you're dropping your child off at another child's home, walk up to the door and meet the parents. Don't drop off your child and just drive away.

Even though most kids want their parents to be less openly involved in their lives as the years go by, you can still stay in touch if you do it diplomatically. Whenever kids are going to a party, call to make sure that one or both parents will be home the entire time. Confirm that no alcohol or other drugs will be available. It only takes a minute, but can save a lifetime of hurt.

Peer group influence can put tremendous pressure on any child. One middle school girl's behavior changed drastically. She went from being a super student and wonderful, outgoing kid to being withdrawn and failing classes. Her parents felt like someone else was living with them, not their daughter. They eventually learned that she was using drugs. She later explained that she felt like she didn't fit in with the popular kids at school so she found a group who did accept her. They did drugs, and so she did, too.

Open your home. Be willing to spring for the pizza, the soda, and the chips, and rent the videos. That way you get to know the kids your kids are hanging around with, and you maintain some degree of control over what they do.

If you feel isolated, connect with other parents of gifted kids. Network! Locate clubs or organizations that share common interests. Organize family centered activities. Make time to be with other adults you enjoy. Work to support your child's school. Other children, as well as your child, will benefit.

Learn More About It

The Centering Book: Awareness Activities for Children and Adults to Relax the Body and Mind by Gay Hendricks and Russell Wills (New York: Prentice Hall, 1992). Great ways to ease stress by relaxing both body and mind.

Gifted Grownups: The Mixed Blessings of Extraordinary Potential by Mary Lou Kelly Streznewski (New York: John Wiley and Sons, 1999). This book takes an honest look at how gifted grown-ups reflect upon their lives.

Growing Up Creative: Nurturing a Lifetime of Creativity by Teresa M. Amabile (New York: Crown, 1992). What to do and what to avoid so your child is free to be creative.

Making Memories: A Parent Home Portfolio by Sally Walker and Lori Whitman (Marion, IL: Pieces of Learning, 1994). An easy step-by-step approach for documenting development and putting together a portfolio for your young child.

Parents' Guide to Raising a Gifted Child by James Alvino (New York: Ballantine Books, 1996). A practical resource for raising and educating gifted children with advice on selecting a school or daycare, tips on promoting intellectual and creative abilities and research skills. Alvino has also written *Parents' Guide to Raising a Gifted Toddler.*

Playing Smart: The Family Guide to Enriching, Offbeat Learning Activities for Ages 4–14 by Susan K. Perry (Minneapolis: Free Spirit Publishing, 2001). A compendium of creative activities that require little preparation for parents and their children.

Talented Children and Adults: Their Development and Education by Jane Piitro (New York: Macmillan, 1998). A comprehensive text on the characteristics and education of the gifted, focusing on factors that encourage talent, from birth through adulthood.

Chapter 4
Coping with Problems

You must be the change you wish to see in the world.
—Mohandas Gandhi

How can I raise a self-confident kid?
How can I understand and cope with my child's super-sensitivity?
How do I deal with perfectionism?
When does normal gifted behavior cross over into the danger zone?
When and how should I get help?

Let's say it right out: Gifted and talented kids are difficult to parent. Right now, you're probably thinking, "That's the understatement of the year!"

Your child is more aware and intelligent, and therefore likely to be more extreme, persevering, and intense than the average child. As a result, you can expect to encounter some problems. This chapter highlights some of the more typical ones, along with a few less common but more serious challenges to guard against.

Possible Problems That May Be Associated with Characteristic Strengths of Gifted Kids

Strengths	Possible Problems
• Acquires and retains information quickly.	• Impatient with slowness of others; dislikes routine and drill; may resist mastering foundational skills; may make concepts unduly complex.

continued

Strengths	Possible Problems
• Inquisitive attitude, intellectual curiosity; intrinsic motivation, searching for significance.	• Asks embarrassing questions; strong-willed; resists direction; excessive in interests; expects same of others.
• Ability to conceptualize, abstract, and synthesize; enjoys problem-solving and intellectual activity.	• Rejects or omits details; resists practice or drill; questions teaching procedures.
• Can see cause-effect relationships.	• Difficulty accepting the illogical, such as feelings, traditions, or matters to be taken on faith.
• Love of truth, equity, and fair play.	• Difficulty in being practical; worry about humanitarian concerns.
• Enjoys organizing things and people into structure and order; seeks to systematize.	• Constructs complicated rules or systems; may be seen as bossy, rude or domineering.
• Large vocabulary and facile verbal proficiency; broad information in advanced areas.	• May use words to escape or avoid situations; becomes bored with school and age peers; seen by others as a know-it-all.
• Thinks critically; has high expectancies; is self-critical; evaluates others.	• Critical or intolerant toward others; may become discouraged or depressed; can be perfectionistic.
• Keen observer; willing to consider the unusual; open to new experiences.	• Overly intense focus; occasional gullibility.

continued

Strengths	Possible Problems
• Creative and inventive; likes new ways of doing things.	• May disrupt plan or reject what is already known; seen by others as different and out of step.
• Intense concentration; long attention span in areas of interest; goal-directed behavior; persistence.	• Resists interruption; neglects duties or people during period of focused interests; stubbornness.
• Sensitivity and empathy for others; desire to be accepted by others.	• Sensitivity to criticism or peer rejection; expects others to have similar values; need for success and recognition.
• High energy, alertness, eagerness; periods of intense efforts.	• Frustration with inactivity, eagerness may disrupt others' schedules; needs continual stimulation; may be seen as hyperactive.
• Independent; prefers individualized work; reliant on self.	• May reject input of parents or peers; nonconformity; may be unconventional.
• Strong sense of humor.	• May appear scattered and disorganized; frustrations over lack of time; others may expect continual competence. Sees absurdities of situations; humor may not be understood by peers; may become "class clown" to gain attention.

From "Mis-Diagnosis and Dual Diagnosis of Gifted Children: Gifted and LD, ADHD, OCD, Oppositional Defiant Disorder" by James T. Webb, Ph.D., *Outlook*, Minnesota Council for the Gifted & Talented, July/August, 2001, p. 12. Used with permission of the author.

You can take some comfort from knowing that research on anxiety, depression, and suicide in academically or intellectually gifted students refutes the notion that these children are at greater risk for problems with adjustment. They, like anyone, encounter problems, some magnified by their gifted characteristics.

Gifted students are diverse in terms of their social competence, just as they are diverse in their gifts. Some gifted kids are skilled at managing their feelings, making friends, negotiating solutions, and cooperating with classmates and teachers. Others may have problems in these areas. Verbally precocious students may have more difficulty getting along socially than those who are mathematically advanced. Students with a higher degree of creativity may be more vulnerable to not fitting in with peer expectations. The more a gifted child feels different, the more difficulty he has adjusting socially.

People react to giftedness in a variety of ways. The reactions can be positive or negative depending on several factors, including the type and degree of giftedness, the fit (or lack of fit) between the child and the educational program, and the child's personal characteristics. Academically or intellectually gifted students who are achieving well and participating in special programs for gifted students are at least as well adjusted—and maybe better adjusted—than other children their age.

How to Raise a Self-Confident Kid

Most of the time, gifted kids get along well socially. But their unusual interests, independence of thought, and nonconforming behavior may give them (and you) some uncomfortable moments. These traits occasionally appear abrasive to others, both children and adults. Legions of youngsters who haven't figured out the current formula for fitting in get labeled as odd or nerdy by their peers.

> *The nerds of today*
> *drive the Lamborghinis of tomorrow.*
> —Carol Brodsky

You can help your child become more skilled at making friends. Discuss with your child why some kids are well liked, so that she can recognize and think about emulating some of these positive traits and behaviors. Also talk gently about behaviors that aren't generally accepted by other kids. If your child often feels left out, find out what she thinks other kids have that she doesn't. Talk about the difference between being popular and being a friend. Popularity is temporary; friendship lasts.

Some children rely on problem behaviors as a way of coping. They do certain irritating things in an effort to boost their self-esteem. If, for example, they believe they *always* have to know the answer and *always* have to be right, their peers are bound to find this abrasive. Some gifted kids feel that they can't ever let themselves be wrong. They feel that to compliment someone else or to acknowledge that a classmate had a good idea somehow diminishes them. These children tend to be stingy about complimenting or even listening to others. They have trouble sharing the limelight, and other children notice this.

Sometimes bright children are labeled nerds or geeks because their interests differ from those of their classmates. Unfortunately, no matter how hard they try, some of these kids are always going to have a tough time fitting into certain social groups. For them, the trick is to find groups they can fit into, or to find one or two really good friends—probably other smart, creative youngsters—who understand and accept them.

Gifted students frequently suffer from feelings of isolation. This can be especially painful during their teen years, when peer approval is so important. Teens want desperately to be like everyone else, from their haircuts to the labels on their jeans. With some bright kids, this happens as early as third or fourth grade, rather than the more usual middle-school years. The person who thinks differently can feel alienated at any age.

Gifted teens who feel like social failures may give up and focus only on their mental abilities. Although kids shouldn't be pushed into social situations that are excessively uncomfortable, everyone's life needs some balance. You may want to encourage your child to at least keep an open mind about making friends. Even socially well-adjusted gifted kids may maintain fewer social contacts than some other teens, limiting their interactions to people with similar interests and abilities.

Ways to Help Your Child

- Share books about other successful nonconformists. Biographies can help a bright young person see that eminent people have had to work hard and struggle in order to overcome problems. That can make the child's own life seem more manageable. Inventor George Washington Carver, born into poverty, wanted to read more than anything. Artist Mary Cassatt was told that she could not paint because she was a woman.

- Help your child find a pen pal or join special-interest clubs, such as a chess club, model car club, or Mensa (a national organization for people with high IQs). Your state gifted coordinator or gifted association might be able to point you toward other possibilities, including organizations of parents like you with kids like yours.

- Enroll your child in a Saturday or evening class that he might enjoy. Sometimes local universities offer special children's classes. Chances are your child will meet others with similar interests and make some connections.

- Volunteer with your child. Give your time and energy to a cause you both believe in. You'll meet others with a similar passion who also are willing to give.

How kids feel about themselves is the real key to social adjustment. Self-esteem begins at home and develops best in an emotionally healthy family. It can be further fostered in gifted classes at school.

Flash! Gifted Classes Boost Self-Esteem!

- "I have an eighth grader whose mathematical giftedness was apparent by age four. Just as apparent by this age were his speech and language difficulties. The gifted math program bolstered his confidence and gave him the opportunity to shine in an area where he excelled. It also helped him accept his verbal difficulty with an attitude of 'you can't be good at everything.' It is important to recognize the fact that within an individual can be found an area of giftedness as well as learning disabilities."

- "My son had all sorts of problems in early elementary school. He was picked on by the other kids, teased, and ridiculed. One day he was even beaten up on the playground. We knew we had to do something. We removed him from his neighborhood school and placed him in a school for the gifted. That school made all the difference for him. Being in the gifted program healed him, made him whole and changed him as a person. He developed self-confidence and communication skills. I will be forever grateful to the teachers and the program for understanding my son and giving him what he needed to succeed."

Dealing with Sensitivity

Gifted kids tend to be sensitive, and some are *super*-sensitive in specific areas. Sensitivity is precious. If nurtured, these sensitivities can develop your child's sense of altruism and service to humankind. The twentieth-century Polish psychiatrist and psychologist Kazimierz Dabrowski used the term *overexcitability* to describe the sensitivity and intensity. He believed that some people are born with the ability to experience life more intensely. Not all gifted children have overexcitabilities, but he found that the gifted population contained more people with over-excitabilities than the general population. According to Dabrowski, children who are born with overexcitabilities have a heightened ability to take in and respond to stimuli. They have increased sensitivity, awareness, and intensity.

Dabrowski identified five overexcitabilities: pyschomotor, sensual, intellectual, imaginational, and emotional. Although they are often linked to negative behaviors and problems, they have a positive side as well: joy, beauty, sensitivity, creativity, and compassion. Educational consultant Sharon Lind emphasizes the importance of celebrating the strengths that overexcitabilities can bring. She recommends strategies parents can use in supporting the positive aspects of each:

Psychomotor Overexcitability

Children with psychomotor overexcitability are active and energetic. They love movement for its own sake and have energy to spare. You may have a child who talks compulsively when she feels something intensely or who shows unusual physical activity and need for action. This over-excitability can show up as misbehavior and acting out, nervous habits or tics, or impulsive actions. It may also take the form of compulsive organization, competitiveness, or workaholism. While these children thrive on activity, the people around them can find them overwhelming. Parents and teachers just want them to sit down and be quiet! Some children with psychomotor overexcitability are misdiagnosed with ADHD.

What do you do when your child exhibits some of these traits? Build activity and movement into the child's life. Allow them to do things. Schedule time to talk things over after school and home activities.

Sensual Overexcitability

Children with sensual overexcitability are sensitive to sights, smells, sounds, touch, and taste. They display heightened pleasure or displeasure at sensual experiences. They hurt and feel with intensity and may show an increased and early appreciation for art, music, and language. They delight in tastes, sights, sounds, smells, and textures. You know that old blanket that you want to throw away that your son carries everywhere? He feels the ribbon binding until it has worn away. He smells the familiar odors and hates for you to wash the ugly thing.

Gifted children sometimes have difficulty with sensory overload and have trouble sorting it all out. The sensitivity may make them distractible. When they are tense, children with sensory overexcitability may overeat, go on a buying spree, or try to be the center of attention or withdraw from stimulation. They may complain about wearing wool. It's too itchy. Or want you to cut off the tag inside the clothing. It hurts. So does the crease in the sock. Perhaps they have a favorite outfit that "feels" good and want to wear it continually. Classroom noise may bother them. Cafeteria smells interrupt their work. They become so spellbound with a work of music or art that nothing else exists.

If your child exhibits sensual overexcitability, try to provide an environment that is comfortable, eliminating offensive stimuli when possible. Provide time to delight in beauty. Watch the rainbow or sunset, listen to the rain and watch the snow fall. Listen to classical music. Take your child to the theater. Put on your own dramatic production to let your child be in the limelight. Take a walk in a garden or run her a scented bubble bath.

Intellectual Overexcitability

Children with intellectual overexcitability have incredibly active minds. They question, observe, and read avidly. They want to know the truth! They may have the prolonged ability to concentrate, to think deeply, and to solve problems. Fairness and moral issues are important, whether on the playground or in the larger world. They worry about adult issues without the wisdom that age can bring. What about the homeless man on the street? Can he sleep in our extra bed? What about AIDS? Or poverty? Or war? Or the environment? They are impatient and critical of others who can't keep up or who do not solve the problems they feel so strongly about. They can be brutally honest. At times their excitement about learning and their impatience may cause them to blurt out answers in class.

Children with intellectual overexcitability often turn away from self-concern earlier than their age peers, and become interested in reforming the world. One ten-year-old girl likes to make a wish on the first star she sees each night. But she rarely wishes for toys and clothes for herself. Rather, she fervently wishes for peace on earth. She has also recognized and is able to discuss the fact that overpopulation is a serious world problem.

If your child displays intellectual overexcitability, you may want to help her act on her concerns. Write letters, donate clothes or food to a homeless shelter, start a campaign, or become politically active. Turn worry to action to show your child that she can help. You can model ways to find answers to big questions. Encourage her to evaluate the reliability of sources, analyze, create, and use new information. Teach tact and diplomacy. Her outspoken tendencies may be perceived as too harsh and critical. Help your child practice ways to disagree without being disrespectful.

Imaginational Overexcitability

The fantasy world of children with imaginational overexcitability is rich. They love images, impressions, and metaphor and have the ability to invent, elaborate, dream, and visualize. They may mix truth with fiction to enrich a story. Imaginary playmates may help these children create their own private worlds. They create drama to escape boredom. It is next to impossible for these kids to pay attention in a classroom with a rigid, fact-driven curriculum. They may make up stories, draw, or go off on tangents rather than doing the required work or participating in mundane class discussions. They may delight in *Harry Potter* or other fantasy literature.

For children who sometimes confuse truth and fiction, new information may blend with creative ideas and facts may become hard to sort out. You can help by encouraging them to write down the facts before they become overblown.

These children should be encouraged to use their imagination to solve real problems. Use the ability to see the unusual to promote learning and productivity. Work with your child to create an organizational system that works for him. Traditional methods sometimes fail for children with so many ideas. Help your child put together a portfolio of his ideas for solving problems in a journal, on a tape, or on video. Make sure he has time to daydream and play with ideas.

Emotional Overexcitability

Parents often notice emotional overexcitability first because of the intense feelings, emotional extremes, and strong expressions of feelings it brings. Emotionally overexcitable children have such compassion, empathy, and sensitivity that they form deep, strong attachments to people, places, and things. They are often accused of overreacting or being melodramatic when the intense feelings they have interfere with mundane tasks like doing homework, folding clothes, or taking out the garbage. These kids feel so deeply that they may be prone to physical symptoms such as stomachaches, headaches, or blushing. They worry about death. They may experience depression. Their awareness of their own feelings and feelings of others may cause them to have conflicting feelings about the depth, or lack of it, in a relationship. They are often demanding and difficult to live with.

Children with emotional overexcitability need help with accepting their feelings. You can be a good listener and let them vent. Accepting their feelings without regard to intensity and helping them work through problems facilitates healthy growth. Teach these children to identify physical warning signs like stomachache, headache, or nervousness. Act on these early to cope with situations that might otherwise gain momentum and spin out of control. Learn to anticipate responses and prepare for them. This can help both you and your child.

Dealing with Overexcitabilities

- Many bright kids focus on how they're *different* from their peers rather than how they're *similar.* They forget that they're human beings, just like their peers, and they feel set apart in a negative way. They perceive their differences as weaknesses rather than strengths. As a family, talk about any overexcitable traits you see in yourselves and each other. Cherish the sensitivities in your children and in yourself. By celebrating these special traits, your heritage, and your family, you validate your child's uniqueness.

- Focus on the benefits of your child's sensitivities. Point out the positives and celebrate the joy they bring.

- Provide opportunities for your child to pursue her passion. Allow time for what she loves. Respect her abilities and interests.

- Teach good communication skills, both verbal and nonverbal. In order to thrive, all people need to learn to listen and respond appropriately to others, as well as to express their own ideas. Teach your child basic politeness: how to ask a question, listen, and respond. Also explain nonverbal communication: tone of voice, gestures, facial expression, postures, and dress all play a role in communication. Many gifted young people don't read nonverbal language well and wrongly interpret behavior. These children need to be encouraged to verbalize and share their feelings and concerns *before* they become overwhelmed by them. Emphasize that communication involves being open to sharing feelings and fears. Good communication also means listening to others.

- Help your child recognize the impact she has on others. She may feel strongly but not recognize how someone else perceives her behavior. What impact does she have when she interrupts? I know an excellent portrait artist who, when he looks at other people, notices if their eyes are too close together, their chin is unusually long, their nose is disproportionate to the rest of their face, their eyebrows are too full, and so on. He told me that whenever he tried to explain his perceptions, people would say, "My, but you're critical!" To him, his observations aren't critical at all; they're just his way of seeing. However, he *did* notice a change in his social life when he started being more tactful.

- Teach stress management. Stress is an unavoidable part of life, but gifted children may have to deal with additional stress, because of their increased mental and physical activity and reactions. Help your child first to identify signs of stress (headache, pacing, worry) and then to develop a strategy to cope (talk about the problem with someone, draw, write, exercise, meditate). Make time for fun and for friends who are understanding and supportive.

- Create a safe, comforting environment. Intense people need a haven of safety. Comfort needs vary from person to person. Music, pieces of art, comfortable clothing, and muted colors can calm and sooth.

Intolerance and the Too-Smart Mouth

It has been said that gifted children don't suffer fools gladly, and some of their parents do little better. But even bright kids must learn that there are times when being right isn't important. Good manners and politeness sometimes mean holding your tongue. For example, when Grandpa uses incorrect grammar, as he has his entire life, it's probably better to accept the words in loving fashion, rather than to criticize him.

Some gifted youngsters who are rejected by their peers don't have a clue about how to handle the rejection. You need to teach your child tactfulness and the other social amenities, no matter how high his IQ may be. Teach him the routines of everyday politeness, such as how to introduce himself, write thank-you notes, and keep potentially hurtful comments to himself. Make it clear that there are times and places when asking questions won't offend others and times when they will. Teach him to write his questions down so he won't forget what he wants to ask if asking the question right away might hurt someone who may overhear.

If your child seems to have an especially loud and critical mouth, it may mean that he doesn't feel good about himself. By cutting others down and pointing out everyone else's faults, he may be trying to raise his own self-esteem. He may be saying to you, "Look at *me* and notice how good I am." Just because *you* know your child is gifted doesn't necessarily mean that *he* knows or believes he is. Even when people repeatedly tell them how smart they are, many gifted young people fear that they'll be found out as not-so-bright imposters after all.

Someday soon (if it hasn't already happened), your child may question your religious beliefs. She is looking for answers. She may want to explore alternative beliefs. And she may not accept "Because I said so" as a reason why she should act or believe in a certain way. For example, if your family goes to religious services together every week, she may decide that she no longer wants to go. Her questions deserve to be heard. And she needs and deserves to hear honest answers in return, even if the best you can do is, "Worshiping is something we do together as a family. You're part of our family, and it's important to us that you be there, too. You can make your own decisions about religious observance when you're older."

Because gifted children may see the world as a scary place to grow up in, they may act particularly immature at times. Being babyish is safe. To act grown-up may seem like too much of a burden. One gifted second grader said that he never wanted to grow up: "It's easier to live at home and have everything done for you. I am protected there." One of your goals is to encourage your child to develop his capabilities, to help him feel empowered, and to show him that he can use his mind to solve problems. He needs to learn that hoping problems will go away or pretending that they don't exist won't get him far. Meanwhile, try to take some comfort in your child's idealism and intolerance for injustice—it's the hope of the future.

Too Good: The Perfectionism Predicament

Perfectionism is the need or the desire to do things *perfectly*, which is an impossible goal. Perfectionism can be one of the most destructive problems that some gifted kids face. They can drive themselves (and others around them) crazy trying to achieve some ideal version of success.

Setting high standards is not a bad thing. Meticulous attention to detail is necessary for scientific discovery. Commitment is necessary for excellence. Striving for excellence leads to great achievement, but these efforts should not be confused with perfectionism. Perfectionism involves setting unrealistically demanding goals for yourself that set you up for failure and feelings of worthlessness. If your child acts as though failure (or even the prospect of failure) is incredibly awful and the only way to live is to be perfect, you need to address the problem. It's the child's perception of herself as a failure in the eyes of those around her, even when all evidence shows a high level of potential and success, that is a danger.

What's so bad about perfectionism? To begin with, since perfectionists feel they have to be perfect, they may try to avoid new experiences. They end up limiting their options just to be sure nothing can happen that might reveal their flaws. Trying means maybe failing—judged by their own impossibly high standards—so these kids never achieve a fraction of what they might. They never risk something that isn't familiar or readily doable.

Perfectionism can be a root cause of underachievement. When there's a huge gap between the ideal and what the perfectionist sees herself accomplishing, she may simply give up. Then she can always say she didn't try. A number of bright kids go so far as to drop out of school.

Gifted and talented children need to be taught that learning, by its very nature, means taking risks. Real learning is not always achieved on the first attempt. Sometimes it takes practice, trial and error, and repetition. The hardest idea to get across is that missing a goal doesn't equal failure; instead, it can be an opportunity to grow. That's why it's so important to allow these kids to experience failure within a safe environment. Don't set your child up for failure, but do provide experiences in which she'll have to stretch herself. Be there to support learning and struggle. Compliment the work, the process of thinking that is involved. Be happy even if the grade is not perfect when learning and struggle have occurred.

Be careful to do this in a nurturing, encouraging way. Well-run gifted classes can provide these types of opportunities. When a distraught fourth grader brought home a grade of B, she thought her world had come to an end. Instead of demanding, "Why didn't you get an A?" the wise parent asked, "What did you learn?"

You can do a lot to keep your child from suffering the pangs of perfectionism. When you focus on the negative or talk constantly about how important it is to make the grade, grow up, get ahead, or do better, you're putting pressure on her. Some kids respond by procrastinating on the easy tasks to avoid harder ones. In fact, some perfectionist gifted kids work so slowly that it drives teachers and parents to distraction. Others may procrastinate by postponing work, again hoping to avoid failure. Let your child know that you understand her desire to do well and recognize her fear of goofing up. Then work at making your home an emotionally safe place for exploring new topics and ideas. Help her to organize and manage her time. Set goals so that the last-minute thrown-together project has been broken into manageable parts with realistic time lines for the separate goals.

A gifted child may rip up paper after paper because her writing or drawing doesn't look like the example in the book. For these children, coloring books discourage their creativity because the perfectly prescribed form is already there. It's preferable to allow these children to experience the real object and draw their own impressions. Show them several master artists' concepts of a subject so they can observe for themselves how varied creative expression can be. The more you let them know that you value uniqueness and originality, the more free they'll feel in their own efforts.

If you're in awe of your child's amazing abilities, you may unknowingly be contributing to a pattern of nonstop reaching for more and higher and better. How? By praising every milestone, every action, every day. Sure, praise can be positive, but not if it's constant. Sometimes this can bring about an unhealthy response.

For example, if you praise your child for every accomplishment, does the absence of your praise on a particular occasion mean you don't appreciate what she's just done? Not necessarily, but she might think it does. Suppose you're in the habit of saying, "Honey, you look nice today." Seems innocent enough, doesn't it? But if you say it every day except one, simply because you forget to say it that day, your child might assume that there's something wrong with the way she looks.

Because bright kids do most things well, it's easy to fall into a pattern of praising without thinking. Your child could end up feeling pressured to keep doing well and fearful that she won't be able to keep it up over the long term. People who are praised too much sometimes believe that they're valued only for their accomplishments, not for themselves.

Does this mean that you should stop praising your child? Of course not. Just concentrate your good words on your child's *efforts*. Say, "It looks like you're really excited about this report," or "Isn't it fun that you get to learn so many interesting new things while working on this project?" Compliment the work in process, not just the finished product.

Whatever you do, don't go in the opposite direction. Criticism is a sure killer of initiative, creativity, and imagination. Resist the temptation to say "I told you so" or "You should have known better." It's much more helpful to say, "What can be learned from this?" (as long as you don't say it in a patronizing way that disguises "I told you so" feelings).

Some children never forget an ill-timed criticism. I know I'll never forget this one: In the first grade, we were supposed to draw a picture of a red barn. I made mine pink because I wanted it to look weathered. I can remember the teacher saying that my barn wasn't as good as the other kids', and not putting it up on the board because it was pink. But there was a logical explanation!

Put-downs vs. Positives

How do you talk to your child? When it's time to point out a problem or a fault, are your words constructive or destructive? Encouraging or discouraging? Here are some common parental put-downs—and positives to try instead.

Instead of this:	Try saying this:
"What happened here?"	"How do you feel about your report card?"
"I expect you to get straight A's."	"Did you learn some new information? What was the hardest thing you had to do?"
"Why can't you do it right?"	"You do a good job of . . ."
"You still can't do . . ."	"You've really improved in . . ."

continued

Instead of this:	Try saying this:
"Why don't you ever . . . ?"	"I like it when you . . ."
"Go look it up."	"Let's find out together."
"That was a dumb thing to do!"	"So you made a mistake. What did you learn from it?"
"Act your age."	"I understand how you feel."
"Are you still working on that?"	"Keep trying. I can see that you're really working hard. Perseverance pays off."

Some gifted children show extreme concern about their appearance. Even young gifted kids may get unreasonably upset when their hair won't behave. They want the image they project to be as perfect as can be, for they believe if they look perfect, they may become perfect.

Some bright children show their perfectionism by becoming extremely anxious before tests. Perhaps they think that if they fail, others will discover that they don't know as much as they've been given credit for. They fear that they will be looked upon as impostors. To them, even an A- is a failure.

One way you can help your child avoid the perfectionist trap is to make sure that the tasks they are given (at home and at school) are neither too hard nor too easy. Tasks that are too easy can lead to poor work habits and the assumption that everything will always come easily. Some gifted kids breeze through high school but flunk out of college for this reason. On the other hand, children who are given tasks that are too difficult or not clearly defined may simply give up. Like most young people, gifted children do best when an assigned task is a little above their ability level. Given *slight* frustration, they have to reach. And that's how they grow.

Be careful not to fall into the trap of doing tasks for your children. That tells them that they are not good enough alone, and they may become overly dependent on you.

Sometimes the best thing you can do for a budding perfectionist is *listen*. Offer a calm comment when you see your child suffering frustration. Say, "You'd like that to be finished perfectly," or "You're really struggling. I appreciate your effort." Remind your child kindly that *everyone* fails on occasion—that it's okay. Keep your eyes peeled for biographies of top achievers. They'll help prove to your child that struggle and even failure often come before great accomplishment. Look at how many discoveries and inventions were "mistakes." Did you know that Post-it notes, microwave ovens, dynamite, stainless steel, and even raisins and coffee are all the results of mistakes?

For example, Thomas Edison tried fifteen hundred different filaments for the light bulb before finding the right one. After the last experiment, an assistant asked, "Well, Mr. Edison, how do you feel about having fifteen hundred failures to your credit?" Edison replied, "They weren't failures. We now know fifteen hundred light bulb filaments that don't work!"

Even if you and your child's teachers aren't applying overt pressure, your gifted youngster may still be plagued by internal stress and strain. Some perfectionist kids develop ulcers, tics, or nervous disorders if they don't find suitable outlets or releases for their tension. Exercise, relaxation techniques, meditation, good eating habits, fun, and laughter all help.

The perfectionist has a low tolerance for mistakes. Instead of being proud of completing a task or running a race, the bright child may only notice that she didn't win any prizes or break any records. Set realistic goals for yourself, and help your kids do the same. Learn to relax yourself. Model acceptance of your own mistakes, showing that you're not crippled for life by an error.

Help your child distinguish between times when it's important to give your all, and times when it's best to just let go. Some tasks are not worth doing well—they're routine jobs that just need to be done. For me, dusting is one of these tasks. I don't like to live in a dirty house, but it seems that no matter how frequently I dust, a film or residue appears on my end tables. I clean weekly, but in the whole scheme of things, other matters take priority in my life. Similarly, I teach my children to set priorities in their lives. Determine what is truly important and go for it!

What's most important is to model nonperfectionist behavior yourself. If you don't have time to clean the house before company arrives, it may be momentarily upsetting, but it's not a life-threatening crisis. If you make a mistake at home or at work, talk about it and let it be known that it's not the end of the world. Disappointments and failures, large and small, are a natural part of life. They help us learn.

When to Worry

How can you tell when one of your child's problems has gotten out of hand and it's time to call in the cavalry? Occasionally it's worth the effort to seek out a school psychologist, therapist, or some other professional who has seen and dealt with similar situations before. But the dividing line isn't always obvious between "It's just a passing phase" and "Uh-oh, this has gone too far and has been going on too long."

Listen to the suggestions of school personnel. Be ready to hear both positive and negative things about your child—without trying to rationalize or defend his behavior. School officials often complain that many parents deny problems that are plainly present. Accurate records are important in helping to solve a child's problem. School personnel and families alike should document the time, the place, and the upsetting behavior.

Ten Tip-Offs to Trouble

How can you tell when something beyond the regular and routine is happening in your child's life—something that may cause real problems, now or later?

Here are some danger signs to watch for. Don't ignore them! When you deal with difficulties early, they don't become unmanageable. And if it turns out that you were worried over nothing, allow yourself a sigh of relief.

1. Self-imposed isolation. Start to worry when your child spends all of her time avoiding you, the rest of the family, and every kind of social situation, even ones involving friends she used to like. It's normal for young people to shut themselves in their rooms for long periods, but it's usually to talk privately on the phone with their friends. If your child seems to spend most or all of her time alone, consider this a warning sign. Try to find out why. Keep computers and televisions in an area of the home where the whole family can use and enjoy them rather than giving kids another excuse to isolate themselves in their rooms.

2. Extreme perfectionism. If the only tasks your child enjoys are those he can do perfectly, and if he's not willing to take a single risk or try anything new, this is a degree of perfectionism you can't ignore. Also be alert to the child who gives up easily and won't try anything at all because he lives in terror of failure. Either way, he's probably miserable and could use some help.

3. Deep concern with personal powerlessness. We all need to feel that we have some influence on the world and what happens to us. The gifted child who feels utterly powerless also feels pain and anger. When she's convinced that she can have no effect on adult situations or world events, she feels helpless and useless. She may strike back by developing a negative attitude or an undercurrent of anger, or by name-calling or putting down others. She may begin distrusting adults and "the system."

4. Unusual fascination with violence. Violence is often glamorized in our culture. Our media exposes us to world events in a way that past generations did not experience. Bright kids know about the atrocities that occur. They may see violence firsthand, far more than they can comprehend and deal with, and TV, movies, and computer and video games can exacerbate overexposure to violence. Some children tune it out; others become fascinated with it.

Don, a bright boy who learned by doing, was such a case. His parents were used to his constant questions and experiments. Yet they noticed a change sometime after he began bringing home dead animals to dissect. At first, he was led by pure scientific curiosity. Gradually his interest took a bizarre twist, and he began mutilating and torturing animals. Cruelty to animals is a warning flag.

In *Smart Boys*, authors Barbara Kerr and Sanford Cohn discuss the volatile condition that is created when intense feelings of alienation are mixed with the intensity of giftedness in a culture with violent influences: "Eric Harris, who with Dylan Klebold, shot and killed teachers and students at Columbine High School on April 20, 1999, in Colorado, was an honors calculus student. Like most high schools, the social pressure to fit in at Columbine was strong. He was known as a geek, and he hated his reputation. He was exposed to violence in the media, and he began to spend large amounts of time focusing on violence. He became fascinated with white supremacist literature, and he used his considerable intelligence to research everything he could about this philosophy, as well as about how to create instruments of killing." The Unabomber, Ted Kaczynski, was a mathematical genius. At a young age, he was exposed to severe punishment and criticism. He created mail bombs that killed three people and injured twenty-three others during his two decades of terror.

5. Eating disorders. In our society, thin is generally considered beautiful. It's not hard to understand why girls in particular may become obsessed with being very slender. When they fear that a single additional ounce will make them less attractive, some may go so far as to starve themselves nearly to death. This disorder is called *anorexia nervosa.* Even if the girl is actually quite slender, in her mind's eye she sees FAT. Although once thought to be primarily a female affliction, anorexia is being diagnosed more and more in boys. The athlete who feels that "fit is not fat" or the skier who knows that "fat doesn't fly" may succumb to eating disorders.

Take Ann. Her slender older sister is a cheerleader, homecoming queen candidate, and all-around good student. Ann wishes she could be like her sister. Although Ann is a good student, too, she doesn't view herself positively. She sees herself as fat, although at fourteen she's a trim ninety-five pounds. So she decides to diet. "If I don't eat, I won't gain weight," she tells herself. But soon, not gaining weight isn't enough—she wants to *lose* weight. She's sure that if she does, others will like her more. The pounds don't come off soon enough for her, and her parents become upset with her for not eating. They insist that she eat, and so she does, only to go into the bathroom and throw up afterward. She may even binge eat and then regurgitate, which is typical of people with *bulimia.*

Tim, on the other hand, is a compulsive eater. Rather than starve himself in a quest for physical perfection, he defends himself against the world by seeking comfort in food. He can eat a dozen donuts, a large pizza, and a gallon of soda before he realizes how much he's consumed. He stashes food in his room, his backpack, and his locker. If he concentrates on eating during lunch, he doesn't have to notice that he always eats lunch alone.

If your child has an eating disorder, you're not at fault, but you do have a powerful role to play in your child's recovery, and you can help in preventing the disease. Recognizing the warning signs is essential. The disease may already be entrenched by the time you see the obvious signs, such as rapid weight loss, compulsive exercising, regularly skipping meals, and disappearing into the bathroom during or after meals. Knowing the early warning signs may allow you to get professional help in a timely and effective way. Eating disorders are not about food itself, but the misuse of food to solve emotional problems. You may notice the less-obvious warning signs of eating disorders in emotions, behaviors, and attitudes that do not directly concern food and eating. Early signs cluster around:

- problems with self-control or self-esteem

- behavioral excessiveness or inflexibility

- either-or thinking

- difficulty dealing with stress

- fatigue, depression, loss of motivation, and social withdrawal

- body image concerns

- difficulty resolving problems courageously and effectively

Parents can play a role in helping to prevent eating problems by modeling balanced eating and exercise at home. Set a regular time when you prepare meals and enjoy them together as a family. Talk about thoughts and feelings openly. Respond to your child's feelings, not the food she eats. Learn as much as you can about eating disorders, and educate your child as well.

If your child does have an eating disorder, be realistic in your expectations for yourself, for your child, and for the professionals helping you. Treating eating disorders is not an exact science. Participate fully in family treatment programs. Set goals that help you stay focused and productive. Make changes along with your child. Know that your child deserves the best help, and make sure she gets it.

6. Substance abuse. Gifted kids feel many pressures: to be accepted, to excel, to change the world. When the pressure becomes too great, it's natural to seek a release. Healthy releases include exercise, meditation, relaxation techniques, and so on. Unhealthy releases include using alcohol and other drugs. Gifted kids may feel that drinking or using drugs poses no problem to them—since they are smart; they know how to handle drugs.

Jerry was a good student, well liked and talented in gymnastics. He worked hard to perfect his skills, spending all of his free time in the gym practicing routines. All was well until he began junior high at a new, large school where he had few friends. Jerry felt left out. When a group of kids who smoked offered him a cigarette one day, he accepted. Smoking with these kids made him feel important, even though it went against his training.

Gradually Jerry started joining his new friends in smoking marijuana as well. The high he achieved resembled the high he worked so hard to get in gymnastics, only it came easily. He became accustomed to this easy high, until eventually his parents noticed that something was wrong. Jerry's grades had dropped drastically. He withdrew from family activities, preferring to spend long periods of time alone in his room. Then his parents discovered that he was skipping classes. They finally realized that Jerry was using drugs and sought help for him.

7. Preoccupation with self. Narcissism has existed through the ages. With the media and ads promoting physical beauty as the sure route to acceptance, love, and happiness, some youngsters overdo their concern about their appearance.

Of course kids should care about how they look, and plenty of youngsters spend hours in front of the mirror. However, if you suspect that your child is taking this too far, check with other parents. How much time do their kids spend primping in front of the mirror and worrying about their clothing? Start considering it a problem when the behavior interferes with normal functioning, or when your child seems to be thinking *only* of himself.

8. Withdrawal into a fantasy world. When the real world feels too threatening, gifted children sometimes withdraw into their own make-believe world. Sam was an extremely bright lad. When he was little, his imagination never shut down. He held onto the tooth fairy longer than most children. He wanted to know about her travels and what part of the world she had last visited. His creative stories were works of art. Sam was very attached to his grandmother. When she died unexpectedly, his mother and father noted how his behavior changed. He talked to imaginary friends, left notes and messages for them, and withdrew from reality. He experienced headaches. When his grandmother's belongings were sold at an auction, his parents thought Sam would have a breakdown. His grief was intense and long lasting.

9. Rigid, compulsive behavior. Some gifted kids refuse to do anything but study. This compulsive behavior pattern often starts because they're having serious difficulties finding anyone they can relate to intellectually. Since highly gifted students think differently from most other kids in their neighborhood or school, and they sometimes lack social skills, they may have a hard time making friends. So they choose to withdraw to their books.

Ali astounded adults as a young child. She had a vocabulary larger than she was, and read on her own by age three. When faced with rules and regulations, she argued like a lawyer and worried about fairness. Temper tantrums and emotional outbursts were also part of her personality. When Ali entered school, she thought that her peers were silly and unknowing. She appeared bossy and controlling to them: she dictated what they should do and when they should do it. Her teacher had to remind her that she was in charge, not Ali. None of this lead to popularity on the playground. She found comfort and companionship in books. They became her best friends.

Another kind of rigid, compulsive behavior is almost the opposite of Ali's. Some gifted and talented kids are superachievers—overscheduled children who are busy, busy, busy. They select impossibly demanding course loads and fuss over the details of schoolwork and extracurricular activities to make them perfect. As a parent, you're thankful when they're old enough to get themselves to all of their activities. You may not catch on that something's amiss with these youngsters, because they seem to be able to do everything and keep it all in balance. They get top grades, excel at sports, run their own small businesses, and still find time to win the lead in the school play. The way to succeed is with superhuman effort. The trouble is, they may burn out early.

Excessive fatigue or constant illness (one cold after another, mono) is a telltale sign that all is not well. If you've got a Superkid, you may need to limit the number or kinds of activities he participates in, for his own good. Value him as a total person, not just for his activities or what he does.

10. Preoccupation with death. *Never, never* ignore this warning sign! The statistics about the rise in teen suicides and attempted suicides are shocking and tragic. It's estimated that six thousand teens end their own lives each year, and ten times as many try. These numbers could be on the low side, since many families don't talk about it when their kids try to kill themselves.

People with above-average intelligence are not at greater risk of suicide than the population as a whole, but particular characteristics may place them at a higher risk for self-destructive behaviors, suicide included. Suicide victims almost always suffer from depression. Depression needs to be dealt with by professionals who can examine the causes and suggest intervention strategies. Oversensitivity can lead to warped ideas and a distorted personality that cause people to lash out in pain. It can also lead to feelings of hopelessness and despair, and even suicidal thoughts. Highly creative, perfectionist males who are pessimistic and obsessive may appear to be depressed, and are at risk. Perhaps because they have such high expectations of themselves and others, they're often perfectionists who perceive failure everywhere (which contributes to a feeling of powerlessness). They begin to believe that failure is so humiliating that life is not worth living.

High creativity can also lead to isolation, isolation can lead to depression. The relationships of gifted individuals are often unusually intense. At an early age, gifted kids question the meaning of life. With the absence of answers can come the feeling of despair. All this adds up to a need for help. Boys are more likely than girls to believe that they have no support system.

If your child exhibits any of these signs of a teen in trouble, get help quickly:

- sudden changes in personality, behavior, eating, or sleeping habits

- alcohol or other drug abuse

- lack of interest in planned activities, withdrawal from family or friends, self-imposed isolation

- severe depression that lasts a week or longer

- concealed or direct suicide threats

- talking about suicide, either jokingly or seriously

- preoccupation with death and death-related themes

- giving away prized possessions

- feelings that life is meaningless

Check your local yellow pages under Crisis Hotlines or Suicide Hotlines to find help.

How to Get Help

At some point in your child's life, she may benefit from a few sessions with a counselor. Studies have found that gifted kids may need more than the usual amount of guidance to achieve and maintain good mental health. A competent counselor can help your child understand and value those differences that set her apart from her peers. Talking helps!

Don't wait until there's a crisis, since counseling often helps students stay mentally healthy and productive. It takes much less time and energy to resolve a problem before it gets out of hand. If your child is having difficulties in school, with peers, or with unusual stress, a counselor can help bring the problem into focus. That's half the battle.

If your child is exhibiting any of the warning signs described earlier in this chapter, the time to get help is now. But where can you go to find it? Although counselors should be available as early as elementary school, they seldom are. Check with your child's school to learn what mental health resources are available. If it doesn't provide counseling services, or if counseling time is so limited that the help is minimal, you may need to seek outside assistance.

Unfortunately, some people still feel there's a stigma attached to seeing a counselor. If your child had a reading problem, would you hesitate to see a reading specialist? A counselor, like a reading specialist, is someone who can genuinely help your child. A trained outsider can see problems you may not be able to see because you're too close to them. A third party can provide an objective point of view. A counselor can also provide you with reassurance that you're doing okay as a parent, or suggest changes that could help your child. And your child will come away with tools she can use to recognize and solve problems, make better choices, raise her self-esteem, and feel more confident about herself and her place in the world.

You can get counseling from a psychiatrist, a psychologist, a psychiatric social worker, or a family therapist. All have different degrees and different types of training and experience. In shopping for a counselor, start by asking friends or school officials for suggestions. The school psychologist or gifted program coordinator may have some recommendations. Your family doctor or pediatrician may be able to refer you to someone. You can also contact your local county department of mental health and your local chapter of the Mental Health Association for referrals.

Be sure to check your insurance ahead of time to find out about coverage for mental health services. Be prepared, however: Few policies cover more than a portion of the costs. And some health plans may insist that you use only the counselors on their approved list.

Before you make the first appointment, it's wise to find out how the counselor feels about issues that are critical to you. Do you have the same or similar values? What are his or her views on giftedness? Does he or she understand the characteristics and implications of giftedness?

Does he or she have experience working with gifted and talented kids? Look for someone who seems relaxed, confident, knowledgeable, and supportive. If you feel comfortable with this person, chances are your child will, too.

Some professionals may suggest that the entire family come in for counseling. Keep an open mind: involving the whole family can't hurt, and it almost certainly can help. Some children may feel better about counseling if other family members are present. On the other hand, teens are often less communicative when their parents are around, so therapists will usually see a teen alone first for a few sessions to build trust, then invite the family in when everyone agrees.

What's most important is to choose someone with whom your child feels safe. When this is the case, real helping can happen, and it won't be long before everyone feels the effects.

What Can You Do to Help?

- **Become knowledgeable about the characteristics, needs and issues of gifted children.** They are different. Because of their difference they may experience or feel rejection. Show them that you value and respect them as total people, more than academic achievement and ability. Support them in their efforts. Be consistent and honest. Give them time; don't overschedule. Encourage friendships with others who have similar interests or hobbies. Talk and listen. They need empathy and intimacy. Without this, some suffer in silence only to release their anger and frustration in negative ways.

- **Insist that teachers and counselors get training on the intellectual, social, and emotional needs of gifted students.** With understanding and work, schools can implement appropriate curriculum that fits the needs of their gifted students. Instead of being restrictive, stressful places for gifted kids, schools can be a place for creative problem solving and laboratories of learning.

- **Advocate for appropriate services for gifted children.** Work to support gifted programming in schools. Help to change laws so that appropriate services are not optional for these students.

Learn More About It

A Brief Overview of Dabrowski's Theory of Positive Disintegration and Its Relevance for the Gifted by W. Tillier (1999). A quick summary of Dabrowski's work on over-excitabilities is available online at *members.shaw.ca/positivedisintegration.*

Counseling the Gifted and Talented by Linda K. Silverman (Denver: Love Publishing, 1993). A valuable resource for understanding the social-emotional implications of giftedness.

Fighting Invisible Tigers: A Stress Management Guide for Teens by Earl Hipp (Free Spirit Publishing, 1995). Stress-management and life-management skills for young people.

Guiding the Gifted Child: A Practical Source for Parents and Teachers by Jim Webb, Elizabeth Meckstroth, and Stephanie Tolan (Scottsdale, AZ: Great Potential Press, 1989). This classic is filled with information and parenting techniques to help you live with and value your unique child.

How to Talk So Kids Will Listen and Listen So Kids Will Talk by Adele Faber and Elaine Mazlish (New York: Avon, 1999). This popular book, which has been used for more than twenty years, has excellent communication strategies.

Perfectionism: What's Bad About Being Too Good? by Miriam Adderholdt and Jan Goldberg (Minneapolis: Free Spirit Publishing, 1999). Written for young people, this book can also teach adults a great deal about this common problem.

Stick Up for Yourself! Every Kid's Guide to Personal Power and Positive Self-Esteem by Gershen Kaufman, Lev Raphael, and Pamela Espeland (Minneapolis: Free Spirit Publishing, 2000). Encouraging how-to advice on being assertive, building relationships, and becoming responsible.

Teaching Children Self-Discipline at Home and at School by Thomas Gordon (New York: Times Books/Random House, 1989). An excellent discussion of why traditional rewards, punishment, and praise do more harm than good, plus noncontrolling methods to get kids to change their behavior.

When Nothing Matters Anymore: A Survival Guide for Depressed Teens by Bev Cobain (Minneapolis: Free Spirit Publishing, 1998). A powerful book for teens about the causes and types of depression, the different kinds of treatment and how they help, and how to stay healthy.

When Your Child Has an Eating Disorder: A Step-by-Step Workbook for Parents and Other Caregivers by Abigail H. Natenshon (San Francisco: Jossey Bass, 1999). A guidebook to help parents understand the importance of being involved with professionals in working to heal eating disorders. More resources from the author are online at *www.empoweredparents.com.*

Chapter 5

Programming for the Gifted

*Too often we give children answers to remember
rather than problems to solve.*
—Roger Lewin

How can your child's educational needs be met?
How can you influence the gifted program at your child's school?

Michael bounded into his kindergarten classroom. He told the other children how to line up and organized playtime. He was willing to take over the class. His teacher found him abrasive, as he blurted out answers, corrected her mistakes, and bossed other children around. His excess energy made sitting still impossible. He was disruptive and inattentive to class activities. His teacher thought that he should probably repeat kindergarten to learn how to socialize, but his parents suspected he was gifted. Only after they politely insisted he be tested did the teacher become aware that Michael had exceptional potential.

When special programs are few and far between and modifications in the classroom are rare, gifted children often must entertain themselves while they wait for other children to catch up. Some gifted children adapt to low classroom expectations and so never use their ability to its fullest. Others seek ways to use their ability. Not all gifted children are equally capable of challenging themselves appropriately. Behavior problems, ranging from daydreaming to refusing to go to school, can result when the school curriculum is not sufficiently challenging.

Research tells us that gifted and talented kids often learn in a different way and at a different rate than other children. But they are also distinct individuals who differ from each other in their abilities and interests. Some gifted kids excel in language yet take twice as long to do their math. The standard school curriculum doesn't meet their educational needs.

The whole point of gifted education is to provide children with appropriate educational opportunities that meet their needs so they can reach their potential.

You, as a parent, obviously care about what goes on in your child's school. Bright children who are bored and frustrated in school are in danger of dropping out—mentally, physically, and emotionally. They may rebel and turn to problem behaviors to make class more interesting: smarting off or becoming class clowns. They may learn to underachieve. If they never have to do anything that challenges them, they often end up with poor or nonexistent study and time-management skills.

It's critical for gifted kids to develop self-motivation skills, which they will use throughout their lives. Throughout their school years, there may be times when they surpass their teachers' knowledge level. If they know how to do research and how to learn, they can keep progressing regardless. We want them to love learning and become lifelong learners.

If you enjoyed watching your preschooler get excited by learning, it would be heartbreaking to see her lose that early enthusiasm. Children may have a general sense of being bored and frustrated without knowing why. They don't realize that part of the reason is that they learn at such a rapid rate. They may not understand what's going on, but we as adults do. Appropriate gifted programming can ensure that your child stays excited about learning, the world, and her own possibilities.

Gifted or Dumb?

Some bright children don't understand their own high ability. They know they are different from other kids their age—some realize this very young—but they don't know why they're different. They sometimes jump to negative conclusions. They may even start to think of themselves as stupid or weird. They lack the wisdom and emotional maturity to understand that just because they learn differently or faster, this doesn't mean that others don't like them. It's our job as parents and teachers to get across the message that they are not weird, and that being gifted is a positive thing.

A four-year-old once told me, "I'm really dumb." I asked him what he meant by dumb. "Well," he told me, "dumb means different. I don't think like everybody else." He had a tremendously large vocabulary that set him apart. He would make comments like, "That's preposterous!" Hardly dumb—but definitely different!

When Ian went with his family to visit friends, his mother told him that she wanted him to act like a *big boy.* Disgusted, he told her that he disliked the term big boy, but he would act "mature and responsible." Ian preferred the company of adults to other kids. He had trouble fitting in with his kindergarten classmates.

Doing well in school is no guarantee that your gifted child's potential is being fulfilled. In fact, a kid who's getting straight A's may not be learning very much. You may feel good when your child comes home with straight-A papers, but think again. Is your child being sufficiently challenged? Is she learning anything new? Is she covering new material or just going over material she already knows? Is she having to make an effort, or is she breezing by?

Too often, bright kids can do the required work easily and have no trouble meeting the teacher's basic expectations. The fact that they could be doing much more often goes unnoticed, particularly if they are well behaved. Unless they have the chance to work with more advanced materials, their abilities stay hidden and they lapse into thinking that no effort is needed. When they finally reach a level where they don't already know the information, they may not know how to study. If everything is too easy for too long, they may expect that learning should be effortless, that being gifted means "I don't have to work hard the way other people do." Some gifted students have struggled enormously or dropped out of college because they didn't know how to manage their time and how to study.

One of the problems for gifted kids is that in the typical classroom, the pressure—especially from peers—is to conform and fit in. If gifted kids are especially productive, they may end up with repetition of the same kinds of assignments (sometimes called extra credit), rather than different or more advanced ones. Who wants to do busywork? No wonder so many gifted kids catch on quickly (after all, they're fast thinkers) and slow down.

Younger gifted kids who can't or won't conform to the average level of classroom expectations may simply withdraw. In a sense, they become mental dropouts from learning. While many continue to pursue their education outside of school, through enrichment programs or their own self-directed projects, the pattern has been set: as far as the school is concerned, they are underachievers who have lost their desire to learn.

One twelve-year-old gifted girl put it this way: "In a typical school day, I whiz through my 'extra' classes and plod through the normal ones. Teachers repeat and 'go over one more time' and explain until their once-fresh ideas are almost meaningless. At times, I try to block it out and then get reprimanded for not paying attention. Sometimes it's easier to just let the haze creep over my eyes and reply robot-like. But it scares me—sometimes I feel like I'll never come back."

For all of these kids—different, bored, ignored, withdrawn, underachieving, and in a daze—gifted programming is essential. This chapter presents a number of models for special kinds of education aimed at the gifted and talented. It also suggests some ways you can start having meaningful input into your child's school experience.

Parents Praise Gifted Programs

- "It changed my son's life. He made a friend for the first time."

- "My son lives for Tuesdays! This is his day to be himself without making excuses or explaining why he thought the way he did."

> • "My daughter's confidence grew. She now tells me she would like to teach in the hopes that she might afford young people the opportunities she received in the gifted program. She learned to work hard and to believe in herself."

Making School Better for Gifted Kids

What are the things that can make school better for gifted kids? Four things can help:

1. an education that fits their intellectual level and talents

2. learning with their true peers

3. a supportive, responsive learning environment

4. professionals who can respond to their needs

Gifted Kids Need an Education That Fits Their Intellectual Level and Talents

Because gifted kids often think, learn, and react differently than the general student population, they require a curriculum that is appropriate to their needs, just as special education students do. Gifted students need and deserve to learn something new every day, to be challenged, and to be understood and valued within the classroom. The regular curriculum must be adjusted or differentiated in order for this to happen.

To download the reports *Regular Classroom Practices with Gifted Students* (Research Monongraph 93102) and *Why Not Let High-Ability Students Start School in January?* (Research Monongraph 93106) visit *www.gifted.uconn.edu/nrcgt/resource.html.*

Research conducted by the National Research Center and the Department of Education shows that many gifted elementary school students have mastered 35 to 50 percent of the curriculum in five basic subjects before they even begin the school year and that most class-room teachers make few, if any, provisions for talented students.

Some educators point out that good educational programming for gifted students is good for all students. And this is true to an extent; all students should be taught to think critically and creatively and to do research and independent study. The difference, however, is that gifted students can handle more complexity, greater depth, and faster pacing than their classmates can. A curriculum that truly meets the needs of gifted students would leave many classmates struggling.

Many educators argue that by differentiating the curriculum—providing different learning activities tailored to meet individual student needs—all students can be accommodated in a mixed-abilities class-room. This can be a solution. However, most classroom teachers, faced with ever-increasing class size and responsibilities, are not equipped to provide individualized or small-group curricula at many different levels simultaneously and consistently. Finding appropriate instruction for a talented student can be a challenge, especially during the early years.

Gifted Children Need to Find True Peers

The higher their level of ability, the more difficulty gifted children face in forming friendships with true peers—children of like interests and abil-ity. A six-year-old child with an IQ of 180 is intellectually almost on a level with an eleven-year-old, and at age ten or eleven is probably equal to the average high school graduate. But in other areas, the gifted child may not be so advanced. His physical development might be accelerated no more than 10 percent and social development 20 to 30 percent. The result is one of the most difficult problems of social adjustment that can happen. The younger and less mobile the child is, the bigger the problem.

Many gifted children say they feel greater peer acceptance, social comfort, and self-acceptance when they are in programs that include other gifted students. Gifted students whose schools do not provide gifted programs often must look to special programs outside of school to find their true peers. If this is the situation at your child's school, the responsibility of locating and paying for these programs falls on you.

Gifted Children Need a Supportive, Responsive Environment

In schools, services should be matched to the needs of gifted students by providing a continuum of options. Flexible grouping—grouping that changes based on readiness to learn, interest, or learning style—in all subjects and at all grade levels can help insure that gifted students are able to learn with and from intellectual and age peers with no stigma attached.

The stereotype that gifted children have pushy parents causes some professionals to doubt or minimize parents' perceptions. It also causes some parents to hesitate to ask for what their children need. But the truth is that most parents understand their children well and readily identify their children's exceptional development. They respond to their children's special needs by providing enrichment activities at home and supporting their interests. They listen to their children. There may be times when parents feel helpless to change things, but lending an ear to the student's concerns may be just what the student needs.

Gifted Children Need Professionals Who Can Respond to Their Needs

Because there are so many differences within the gifted population, there is no ideal teacher for these students. It is essential, however, that professionals who work with gifted students be interested in and eager to work with students who are curious and highly able. Gifted children require professionals who understand both their academic needs and their social/emotional needs. Adults who work with gifted children need to understand that the highly gifted child thinks and reacts differently than the moderately gifted child. Likewise, the moderately gifted child thinks and reacts differently than the average child. Schools should select and train staff based on the needs of the gifted students they serve in their programs. Adults need to be prepared to follow these children's minds to unexpected places if they are to really understand and guide them.

How Schools Program to Meet the Needs of Gifted Kids

Educational programming for gifted kids occurs in a number of ways: special schools, enrichment, differentiation within the classroom, acceleration. Because no single program is perfect for all children, gifted or otherwise, schools use a variety of methods in gifted education. These methods may be offered singly or in combination. What works best is a continuum of programming options to meet the needs, abilities, and talents of the children who take part in the gifted program. The following pages discuss some of the common programming options.

Special Schools and Separate Programs

Although this option is rare, some districts offer separate magnet schools for gifted children. Magnet schools—public schools designed to attract students from throughout the school district—are a particularly effective solution, since bright children get to spend all day with each other, instead of just one or two periods during the week. These schools may be popular and have strict entrance requirements and limited space availability.

Other schools group students by ability or readiness to learn—a sort of school-within-a-school. Gifted students attend core curriculum courses taught by specially trained teachers for part of the day and spend time with other students for other classes for the rest of the day. Students with all levels of academic readiness might participate in the same physical education class, for example; but a special math class may be reserved for those students who have the potential to excel.

Enrichment Programs

Enrichment programs are among the most common gifted programming options. They are designed to replace or extend the regular school curriculum. The goal of enrichment should be to help students work on problem solving and higher-level thinking skills, such as analyzing, creating, and evaluating. These skills are often taught through debates, discussions, research, and simulations.

Enrichment programs vary from an hour a week to an hour or more a day, or even a whole day in some schools. Enrichment might involve using a resource room, implementing pull-out programs, offering mentorships, hiring specially trained teachers, inviting community professionals to teach or make presentations, or setting up individual projects or contracts with the student.

The **Future Problem Solving Bowl** and similar competitions offer enrichment opportunities to gifted students. In this program, begun by Paul Torrance in 1975, teams are given a problem to solve. The students do research, list subproblems, and present solutions orally and in writing. For more information about Future Problem Solving Bowl, write: Future Problem Solving Program, 2015 Grant Place, Melbourne, FL 32901; call 1-800-256-1499; or visit *www.fpsp.org* on the Internet.

Resource rooms are usually libraries, computer labs, or other specially equipped rooms that gifted kids use at the teacher's discretion. For example, students who have completed a particular assignment may be allowed to go to the resource room to research an area of interest or work with the librarian or other specialist.

Resource rooms can be havens for gifted kids—places where they can make new friends of similar abilities, work on fascinating projects, and use specialized equipment. Usually the teachers who work in these rooms are sensitive to the needs of the gifted and talented and not threatened by students who often know more than they do about certain things. Some gifted resource rooms are separate entities, while others may share space with the LD resource room or even the school library or computer stations.

Sometimes, however, when the use of the resource room is determined solely by the classroom teacher, many students who could benefit from it never get sent there. And some may be able to use it only at the teacher's discretion—as in, "You haven't done the assignment. You don't deserve to go there." Ideally, resource rooms shouldn't be used as punishments or rewards. They should be available to students who *need* them.

Pull-out programs remove gifted kids from the regular classroom for a period of time. They usually provide special activities not offered in the regular classroom, on a part-time basis. For example, some deal with emotional and social competencies or thinking skills not covered in the regular classroom. Pull-out programs can vary from an hour a week to several hours a day to an entire day, though the latter is rare.

For pull-out programs to be effective, they must be coordinated with the regular curriculum. The pull-out curriculum must have substance. Pull-out activities may be fun, yet they should offer appropriate learning activities that relate to the rest of the student's curriculum. Some districts that start their gifted program with a pull-out program become complacent and fail to develop more comprehensive programming later on. One hour a week is not sufficient programming for students who are gifted all day, every day.

Another drawback of pull-out programs is that students may miss important or fun events that happen in their regular classroom. What if there's a test the next day on material presented while they were in the pull-out program? Will they regularly miss recess or special programs? If so, then the gifted program is more of a pain than a pleasure, and children won't be motivated to stay in it for long.

Mentorship programs pair gifted students with an adult or another student who's an expert in a particular subject or profession. Mentors may be older students sharing an area of common interest with a younger mentee or a business professional offering a glimpse at what a particular occupation is like. Usually, students and mentors agree to work together closely on specific goals for a set period of time. Meetings are arranged during or after school hours, as determined by the participants and school staff.

Accelerated and enriched learning are the natural consequences of mentorships. Mentorships also provide good career exploration opportunities and friendships based on interests rather than age.

Independent study allows students to work at their own pace on a program of their own choosing. A mentor or teacher serves as a guide.

Most independent study programs require students to develop a plan stating the subject of their study, list their goals and objectives, plan activities to achieve those goals, and complete a final product. The study plan may take the form of a contract. A product can be the end result, showing what the student has learned.

Gifted Students in the Regular Classroom

Some schools use the inclusion model from special education to include gifted students with everyone else in the classroom.

In a mixed-abilities classroom, students learn in different ways and at different speeds. Gifted kids need less time to learn facts and skills but more time to do something with them. The way many classrooms try to handle this is through differentiating instruction—adapting the class work to students' individual needs. Teachers trained in differentiation techniques are essential. Differentiation can occur in these four areas:

1. Content. Teachers can alter the subject matter or material students learn to allow for greater abstraction, complexity, variety, or organization. They can organize the material to help gifted kids discover or develop a big, broad idea or picture. This capitalizes on the excitement and curiosity of bright students.

Going deeper into the area of study is another way to alter content. For example, the mathematically gifted child who can cover a year's worth of math in a semester might use the extra time to study different number base systems, number patterns, or other concepts that other children her age may not grasp. She could even progress to the next level of difficulty in the math sequence. Teachers need to take care to coordinate with the child's future teachers whenever possible so that she doesn't have to wait for the rest of the class to catch up at some later point.

Another example of differentiating by content might involve looking at concepts from a variety of perspectives. When studying her city, for example, a student might look at other cities and discuss issues in city planning and development, perhaps creating a plan for an ideal city. The student can be encouraged to think like a professional in a particular discipline, learn the vocabulary of the discipline, and discover how the discipline has changed over time. For example: As a historian, how would you feel if your favorite historical building were about to be demolished for a new high-rise? As an entrepreneur who desires a prime business location, tell how you'd feel about building your new business on the spot where the tumbledown relic is now standing. As an ecologist, tell how you'd feel about losing all the green spaces in the city to buildings and cement. Discuss your concerns for the wildlife and its loss of habitat.

Gifted kids need to develop their ability to see the connections among various disciplines. Thematic units or universal concepts are needed for reaching across and making connections between disciplines.

2. Process. Teachers can differentiate the learning process by varying how the content will be studied, what thinking skills students will use, and how students will acquire those skills. Teachers vary the process when they give students the freedom either to choose what method they will use in solving a problem or to come up with their own methods.

Some teachers use Benjamin Bloom's taxonomy of educational objectives to teach kids thinking skills. Bloom's taxonomy outlines six levels of thinking that build on each other in terms of complexity:

- *Knowledge* is the foundation, the facts and details that make the content special.

- *Comprehension* involves showing understanding, being able to state ideas in your own words.

- *Application* is the ability to use what you have learned.

- *Analysis* is the ability to analyze, classify, or compare and contrast two or more things.

- *Synthesis* is the creativity—making something new, trying something never tried before.

- *Evaluation* involves judging or determining the relevance or worth of things.

3. Product. Gifted kids can demonstrate what they've learned in many different ways. Too often, however, teachers expect the final product to be a written paper or a test. But the products of learning should vary.

Offering students a choice among various ways to demonstrate their learning allows them to develop their own learning style preferences. Teachers differentiate products by having students choose to create a product that is oral (speeches, debates, or discussions), written (journal entries, essays, poems, or stories), visual (drawings, story maps, charts, collages), kinesthetic (skits, models, demonstrations), or technological (Web sites, slide shows, videos). Product variety can help fight student boredom, as well as be the vehicle for letting others see how much the student has learned.

Having a range of product choices that spark their interests can help students learn how to do real research. Rather than employing a single method such as going to the Internet to find information on a topic, printing it out, and turning it in, students must transfer relevent information into a different format. They can ask and find answers to specific questions, then think at a higher level and demonstrate their learning in a creative way.

When teachers allow students to create different products, they need to be careful to spell out specific criteria for evaluation and clearly outline the characteristics or expectations. This helps the student to know the expectations at the beginning of the project and avoids surprises in grading.

4. Learning environment. The physical setting where learning takes place can be varied in many ways—for example, moving students to a different location, calling in a teaching specialist, or blending classrooms. The learning environment needs to include appropriate equipment and facilities—essentials like language and science laboratories, computers, video equipment, and so on.

The learning atmosphere should be one of mutual trust, respect, and commitment to self-improvement. Teachers should strive to create a climate that encourages thinking and questioning, respects individual differences, and allows for disagreement and controversy. It must be a safe place, where a student can take risks without fear of humiliation.

Finally, the learning environment must be responsive to gifted kids' feelings as well as their intellectual needs. When this is the case, students can accept constructive criticism, respond creatively, and develop ways to cope in the real world.

Basic differentiation techniques such as compacting and cluster grouping can help teachers meet the needs of gifted kids.

Compacting is a differentiation technique that involves compressing the learning time for students who demonstrate mastery of specific material or skills (usually through a pretest). For example, if a child has already memorized the multiplication tables while most of the rest of the class is still learning them, the teacher could guide her in extending her knowledge at the appropriate pace. With compacting, teachers need to be careful to assure that gifted students spend some time with their gifted peers. Compacting ensures that gifted students do not waste learning time repeating work they've already mastered.

Cluster grouping is another differentiation technique that teachers can use in the regular classroom. It is a commonsense approach to avoid tracking by ability grouping, yet allowing gifted students to be together to enable them to learn in ways that support their strengths. Cluster grouping places gifted kids together into a group of learners with similar abilities and needs while the rest of the class is divided into mixed-abilities groups. This technique works best when the teacher of the cluster group has training in differentiation and curriculum compacting.

Independent study is one way classroom teachers can incorporate skill work while developing higher-level thinking. There's a big difference between memorizing a fact and knowing how to apply it creatively. The program also can be made different (and better) by making it more complex, faster moving, deeper, and more meaningful to the students.

Acceleration

Acceleration allows children to jump to a higher level of schoolwork than their age would ordinarily dictate. Acceleration can take many different forms: early entry to school, placement in a self-contained gifted classroom, earning credit by examination, skipping a grade or more, completing two grades in one year, or concurrent enrollment in both college and high school. It can involve mastery learning, allowing students to progress through the curriculum at their own pace. Or a student might be accelerated by skipping a grade or more in a particular subject. Whole-grade acceleration is usually considered for students who can work at a level two or three years beyond other students their age.

While acceleration is reasonably commonplace, many people are staunchly against it, especially when it comes to early entry and grade skipping. They worry that gifted children who associate with older kids will suffer emotionally. This is worth thinking about. If your youngster skips one of the early grades, what may be the results when high school rolls around and she's the youngest among her peers? She may not be as developed physically, which can affect her participation in sports and other activities. She won't start to drive when her friends do, and she may not be ready to date at the same time as her schoolmates.

Despite these considerations, many studies show that when children are allowed to learn at their own pace, they feel better about themselves, they're more motivated and creative, they have higher aspirations, and they're more socially with it.

Iowa Acceleration Scale Manual: A Guide to Whole-Grade Acceleration K–8 by Susan Asouline, et al. (Scottsdale, AZ: Great Potential Press, 2002). The Belin-Blank Center at the University of Iowa has developed this scale to guide educators in deciding when whole-grade acceleration might be appropriate for a student. It provides educators and parents with scores and guidelines to help them make educated and appropriate placement choices for students who demonstrate high ability and who may need more than they are able to get in their present learning environments.

Advanced Placement

Advanced Placement (AP) classes are college-level classes that offer high school students greater academic challenge, more opportunities for accomplishment, and chances to make individual progress. Sponsored by the College Board, their goal is to prepare students to take a national examination in May that gives them the opportunity to earn college credit while in high school. Although AP classes are not necessarily gifted programming, they are an option that many high schools offer their gifted students. Similarly, high school honors classes are simply higher-level classes and not necessarily gifted classes.

Special Arrangements for College

Some schools offer students dual enrollment in high school and college. Rather than take AP classes at their high schools, students may be excused from regular classes for part of the day to take courses at a nearby college at the school district's expense. Arrangements vary, but students generally receive both college and high school credit for such courses. Often high schools allow this only if they do not offer a similar class in the high school.

Some high schools also allow students to complete the graduation requirements in fewer than four years so they can begin college at a younger age. Students can progress through the curriculum more quickly and flexibly than usual, and sometimes the district will waive required coursework if students have learned the content through home study, travel, or independent study under the direction of a teacher. If they demonstrate mastery, they may receive academic credit.

International Baccalaureate Program

The International Baccalaureate program is known worldwide for its rigor and appeal for students who think globally. The high academic standards and strong emphasis on the ideals of international understanding and responsible citizenship make it unique. Schools authorized by the International Baccalaureate Organisation (IBO) to administer the programs receive assistance in curriculum and assessment development, teacher training, information seminars, electronic networking, and additional educational services.

IB programs are now offered in more than a thousand schools in a hundred countries. Students who have graduated from a high school with an IB program often qualify for advanced courses in college. You can check with your school district to see if any schools in your area offer IB programming, or visit *www.ibo.org* online to learn more about the program.

Internships

Another way for bright high school students to enhance their education is through internships—working with professionals on the job. Internships are usually most available to high school students in the later grades. Some schools have formal internship programs with guidance counselors who match students with professionals in a particular field. Students may get the opportunity to shadow a professional and learn what skills and knowledge a particular job involves. They may have a job-like experience working in many different aspects of a business. Student interns can work with professionals to learn additional skills, network with others in the field, and even explore future work opportunities.

If your child's school does not have a formal internship program, internships can sometimes be arranged privately. Talk with a high school counselor or curriculum coordinator. Schools may regularly offer internship training and experiences in vocational education, but they may not have explored this area for gifted students. Ask and you may open the door.

Evaluation

Ongoing evaluation is essential as a basis for refining, modifying, and recycling any gifted program. This is where your input as a parent is especially valuable. Whether it's formal (such as written evaluations) or informal (such as ongoing comments to the teacher and principal), your constructive ideas for improving the program are vital and should be welcomed. What once worked may not be working now. New materials, ideas, staff, or students may dictate that change is needed.

When asked, "What has made a positive impact on you and your learning?" gifted students replied:

- hands-on learning projects

- service learning activities in community or school

- creative and innovative ways of teaching the curriculum

- curriculum that is meaningful and connected to the real world

- enthusiastic, respectful teachers who love their job and like their students

- outside people coming in to discuss their experiences

- flexible scheduling

Your Rights and What's Right

As a parent, you have the right to know when and how children are being identified for your child's school's gifted program. You also have the right—and the responsibility—to know when tests are being given and what the results are. That way you can talk about these tests with your child so he'll feel more comfortable with what's happening.

You must be informed if your child is participating in a gifted class. Some districts hesitate to tell parents out of the misguided fear that they will get inflated egos. But you need to know so you can understand and support your child.

Unfortunately, the many teacher education programs haven't caught up with research on gifted education. Sometimes teachers themselves aren't sure how to make curriculum and instruction appropriate to the needs of gifted kids. They simply have not had the necessary classes or staff development. Don't hesitate to ask questions and speak up for your child. Chapter 6 gives you some tips that should help you do this.

How do you know whether what your school provides is right for your child? Visit, visit, visit! Position yourself as the teacher's partner, rather than as an adversary. You can say to the teacher, "I have some time—how can I help you in the classroom? I'd like to read a story to the kids; can I share my hobby with the class? Could I help with a bulletin board or pull some resources for you to use?"

One parent took her child's teacher a bagel and coffee on the first day of school as a great beginning. She wrote positive comments to the teacher when the child had good experiences or showed growth. Because of this, the parent felt that her child's teacher was much more willing to hear when something went wrong or to discuss an issue when questions arose. Be positive when you can. We all need positive feedback, and letting your child's teachers know what they do well will help you go a long way.

Rights of Students

By Carol Morreale
For the Illinois Association for Gifted Children

ALL students need and deserve an equal opportunity:

- to stretch their minds around new and difficult curriculum content, maximize their potential, and demand the use of higher-level thinking. Differentiation within classrooms is

continued

important. Gifted students need teachers who modify the curriculum to make it more intellectually demanding. Gifted students need a quicker pace, a greater depth, and more abstract processes. All students need a level of content slightly beyond their grasp, so they will apply higher-level thinking.

- to learn how to learn, which requires organization skills, study skills, and persistence. For gifted students, this occurs only when curriculum is challenging and they are held accountable.

- to feel part of a group and to learn together with intellectual peers for at least part of every school day. Gifted students need to feel connected with age mates, and also with other gifted students. Learning with others of similar ability makes them feel less isolated and more stimulated.

- to have their abilities recognized and challenged early. Any exceptionality requires early intervention to develop full potential. In primary grades, academic rigor is as important as socialization skills. Without appropriate academic challenge for young children, educators may unknowingly ask children to deny who they are.

- to develop their uniqueness in a psychologically nurturing environment. Gifted students sense that their peers are impatient with the depth of their questions, the sophistication of their vocabulary, and the uniqueness of their interests. They need significant adults in their world to accept and assist with social/emotional issues that relate to self-understanding, peer relations, and family relations.

- to be fully engaged in the learning process. Because gifted students often come to class with a broad knowledge base, they wait a long time to learn something new. Professional development and stronger teacher certification requirements are needed for staff to be able to provide appropriate educational experiences that will engage gifted students.

continued

- to be free from discrimination based on intellect, gender, race, poverty or age. Meeting the needs of the gifted should not depend on the community one lives in, or traditional role expectations. For example, gifted students may need earlier access to school or curriculum levels. Gifted females may need encouragement to pursue accelerated math and/or science classes. Students in low socioeconomic areas should have equal access to gifted programming based on local standards.

- to experience the joy of learning and succeeding, a feeling which is contagious, and has life-long positive effects.

"Rights of Students" by Carol Morreale (Illinois Association for Gifted Children, 1993) Used with permission.

What Is the Teacher's Role?

Whatever curriculum model or strategies a school selects, the teacher is the key to your child loving school. The staff has to be involved in the planning stages of the curriculum in order for it to be accepted and successful, and the administration needs to support it. The administration, teachers, and students should work together to develop, implement, and evaluate the curriculum.

The teacher's role is to create a learning environment that's both safe and stimulating. The teacher also helps the students achieve a balance between independent activities and those for small groups and large groups. The teacher serves as a facilitator or guide, rather than as a dispenser of information, while maintaining a focus on the quality of the learning experiences.

Remember that when it comes to actual implementation of the curriculum—the day-to-day reality of teaching—the teacher has the final word. The teacher is the trained professional. It is the teacher who is being evaluated by an administrator on what and how curriculum is taught. Parents do, however, have the right—and the responsibility—to ask questions and insist on appropriate educational programming for their children.

Good teachers of gifted kids must have a desire to teach students who may be brighter than they are, and they must not feel threatened by that.

They should have a love of learning and confidence in their ability to work with students. Good teachers show flexibility and comfort with students doing different things in the class. A sense of humor is a plus.

When bright students were asked to describe a "gifted" teacher, they listed these characteristics:

- someone who understands and respects gifted kids

- someone who encourages kids to set and achieve high goals

- someone who goes into assignments more deeply than the book does

- someone who writes compliments on a student's paper if he or she does a good job

- someone who listens

- someone who is responsible, efficient, innovative, and smart

- someone who is loving and caring

How Parents Feel About Teachers of Gifted Kids

- "My son wanted to drop out of school last year. He feigned illness and looked for excuses not to go. This year, since he is in the gifted program, he has completely changed his attitude about school. He loves going to the gifted teacher and has made new friends."

- "Our son was bored to death with the regular math program. He did not do his homework and refused to do assignments that were too easy and boring. He made careless errors and turned in sloppy papers. This year the school placed him in the gifted pre-algebra class. He loves it! He looks forward to the class, and works like crazy on the assignments. I'd hate to think what would have happened if he had not gotten into this class."

> • "My daughter loves her gifted teacher. She claims that she wants to grow up to be just like her. Her interest in books and her love of learning have blossomed in the gifted program. She now feels that she can do anything she wants to do if she works hard enough."

It takes more time and effort for a teacher to plan, teach, and evaluate lessons for gifted students. Many professionals and parents wrongly believe that teaching smart kids is easy because they learn faster and easier than the average child. Nothing could be further from the truth! Gifted and talented children require more teacher time and effort because of the quantity of work they do, and more teacher training because of the sophistication and quality of that work. They tend to consume more and need more, not just quantity, but quality. It takes advanced reading and work just to keep up with this student. Just by appreciating this truth, you can be supportive of your child's teacher.

Try to make time to help in the classroom or in other ways. Some ways to help include: offering to drive on field trips, doing outside research, making classroom teaching aids, and working with small groups of children on enrichment activities.

Bored No More

Educator Judy Galbraith has identified one of the "great gripes" of gifted kids as, "The stuff we do in school is too easy and it's boring." Students had the following suggestions for making school more challenging:

- "I try to explain to my teacher when I already know what's being taught. She's pretty good about letting me read on my own."

- "When my regular work is done, I ask my teacher if I can work on the computer. I love working on the computer and can occupy myself for hours."

It's a Match!

What happens when gifted kids and gifted programs match—when the curriculum meets the children's needs? Here's what parents have said:

- "My child is finally challenged."

- "My child has developed self-confidence."

- "My child *loves* going to school. She even wants to go on weekends."

- "The classes are work, but fun, too."

- "No longer is my child ridiculed for being a know-it-all. She is with other kids who think on the same level. They accept her for who she is."

When It's Not a Match

In some cases, even though you have worked with the school, had conferences with the teacher, progressed through the levels of decision-makers, nothing is happening for your child. The reality is that some schools do not have the necessary resources or know-how to offer solid programs to meet your child's needs. Where do you go from here? What are your options? This section outlines some ideas you can explore.

Public School Choices

Some public school districts allow students to move from one school to another within the district. Others don't. Some states and metropolitan areas have agreements that allow students to transfer between school districts. Investigate your district's policy, as well as the availability of options such as magnet schools and charter schools. These types of schools have been created to provide families more choices in public education, encourage competition among public schools, and spur innovation and improved educational outcomes for all children.

Magnet schools, which are usually found in large school districts, are specialized public schools that frequently emphasize a particular curriculum, theme, or instructional focus (such as technology, the arts, science, cultural immersion, gifted programming). Students from across the district are eligible to attend, and the district provides transportation to the school. Popular magnet schools may have waiting lists and most have application deadlines. Start investigating early to find out the options available in your community.

Charter schools are public schools managed independently by educators, parents, and other community members rather than a school

board. Like magnet schools, they may be organized around a particular mission, educational philosophy, curriculum, theme, or teaching method. Although they are free from some of the inflexible policies and regulations that most public schools must follow, they must adhere to specific state and federal guidelines, such as laws against discrimination. In some states, charter schools must demonstrate improved student achievement or their charter will be revoked. As is true of magnet schools, parents and students within the district can choose to attend and are limited only by the availability of space. Popular schools may have a waiting list or a lottery for entrance. Before choosing a charter school, look at its philosophy and teachers and be sure to visit the school to make sure it fits your child's educational needs.

Private Schools

Private schools offer a wide array of educational options from religious-based instruction to nonsectarian preparatory schools. The costs of attending also vary widely. Don't assume that a private school will automatically offer your child a better education or one more suited to gifted children than the public schools will. In some states, public school-teachers who teach gifted children must have taken a minimum number of courses in gifted education. This is not so in most private schools. Be sure to ask what happens when children already know the content or information being taught in class. What kinds of curriculum adaptations are available to meet these kids' needs?

Private schools may be able to offer a lot of what you desire, but the cost may be high. Find out what scholarships are available, or if a school that seems like a good fit for your child offers a sliding tuition scale based on family income.

Homeschooling

Some parents prefer to homeschool their gifted children, either full time or part time. Homeschooling involves educating your child outside of the traditional school system, often at home. A parent or mentor directs the child's education with the goal of meeting the student's individual learning needs and offering more challenging and interesting experiences.

Although homeschooling requires a huge commitment of both time and resources, it has many benefits, especially for students who learn at a different pace than other kids their age. Gifted children who are homeschooled find they no longer have to play tutor to their classmates or wait for them to catch up. They also don't have to deal with common classroom discipline problems that take up valuable class time. You can structure the curriculum around your child's learning style, interests, and readiness to learn. You can accommodate your child's sensitivities and her intensity about certain topics. You can explore areas in depth and complexity. You can take field trips and plan projects without restrictions. One parent reported that she loved being able to work with her son on an extended basis. She was able to see his love of learning develop and help him make connections between the concepts he was learning and other areas of his life.

Homeschooling is not easy, however, and it cannot be taken on lightly. Schools have textbooks and written curriculum to follow and teachers with different areas of specialization. Parents who homeschool must either have knowledge of all curricular areas or have access to information and written curricula.

If you are considering homeschooling, consider whether your child will reenter the school environment at some point. Some homeschooled students decide to go to public or private high school because they want to participate in school activities, plays, clubs, AP or honors classes, sports, band, musicals, etc. Some homeschooled students progress in their studies beyond their classmates. Other homeschooled students find holes in their learning once they get to high school.

If your homeschooled student doesn't attend high school, you must ensure that your child's advanced needs are met. Are you prepared to teach other languages, advanced mathematics, laboratory science, or in-depth research skills? Are you knowledgeable about literature and history? Some parents may be better prepared than the schools, others are not. Also consider how you will evaluate and document your child's learning. What are your child's plans for the future?

Some students miss the social interaction that occurs in a regular school. Others don't. Not having the same experiences as the other kids in the neighborhood or not knowing the same people may be a problem for some kids but not others. Some kids miss the sense of independence that comes with going to school. They like to have their own experiences to tell you about. Others like having a parent be their teacher.

If you homeschool your child, you may want to develop a group of other homeschoolers who meet to work on projects, go to a park, attend concerts, visit museums, talk about books, put on plays, or play soccer. Some homeschooling parents form cooperatives to allow their children to explore a greater variety of topics and interests. The parents supplement each other's weaker areas and build on their strengths. For example, one parent may have a background in science and do challenging scientific research projects with several children. Another may be an expert in music and share that talent with the children. The students also benefit from having a variety of adults help structure their learning. It can be hard when Mom or Dad is the only teacher.

If your child has a special need, such as a learning difference or language barrier, consider the special challenges this might present in homeschooling. Public schools have the support of a variety of professionals to help with specific learning differences. For example, a child with a speech impediment might require the assistance of a speech pathologist. If you don't have the expertise or training necessary to assist the child in that area (and how many of us do?), the school may be better able to meet the child's need than you are. A combination of homeschooling and public or private schooling may be best for the child for a time.

Homeschooling is legal in all fifty states, Canada, and many other countries, but laws and policies vary widely. Be sure to check with your local school board or regional state offices so you understand the legalities before you begin. Connecting with other families who homeschool is an excellent way to learn more.

If you have other restrictions or obligations, you might want to try homeschooling on a part-time basis. Work with the school to develop your child's special interest or passion. Use the school's curriculum as the starting place and conduct research and develop a project. Check out Web sites. Try homeschooling during the summer. Discover what works for your child and you.

Recognize that no one program is going to meet all of your child's needs. There are pluses and minuses to all options. You know your child.

What may work for one child does not necessarily work for the next. You have the right and responsibility to explore options and make decisions about what *your* child needs. With patience and persistence you will make progress on behalf of your child.

Learn More About It

Aiming for Excellence: Gifted Program Standards edited by Mary Landrum, Carolyn Callahan, and Beverly Shaklee (Washington, DC: National Association for Gifted Children, 2001). A framework of standards for educators to use when planning programs for gifted students.

A to Z Home's Cool Homeschooling Web Site
homeschooling.gomilpitas.com
This large collection of articles, links, and resources on homeschooling includes a section on homeschooling gifted children, as well as basic information on legal issues.

The Complete Guide to Homeschooling by John and Kathy Perry (Los Angeles: Lowell House, 2000). A guide to homeschooling that includes a comprehensive list of contact information for departments of education and home educator organizations in all fifty states. It can also help you to explore whether or not to homeschool, how to develop confidence and keep life in balance, what to teach, and how to approach homeschooling with elementary, middle school, and high school students.

The Gifted Kids' Survival Guide: For Ages 10 & Under by Judy Galbraith (Minneapolis: Free Spirit Publishing, 1999). A book for gifted kids about what it means to be gifted.

The Gifted Kids' Survival Guide: A Teen Handbook by Judy Galbraith and Jim Delisle (Minneapolis: Free Spirit Publishing, 1996). Information for gifted teens on giftedness, school success, college planning, and more.

Some of My Best Friends Are Books: Guiding Gifted Readers from Preschool to High School by Judith Wynn Halsted (Scottsdale, AZ: Great Potential Press, 2002). A resource guide based on the idea that by reading and discussing books with children, parents and teachers can improve self-awareness and promote nonthreatening discussions.

Teaching Gifted Kids in the Regular Classroom by Susan Winebrenner (Minneapolis: Free Spirit Publishing, 2001). Learn about ways to meet the needs of the gifted child in the regular classroom.

Teaching Young Gifted Children in the Regular Classroom by Joan F. Smutny, Sally Walker, and Elizabeth Meckstroth (Minneapolis: Free Spirit Publishing, 1997). A resource packed with educational strategies to bring out the best in young children.

Chapter 6

Advocacy: Working for Improvement

*Success is knowing the difference between cornering people
and getting them in your corner.*
—Bill Copeland

How can I speak up for my child?
How can I encourage more support and funds for gifted programs and kids?

If you want to make sure that your gifted child receives the best education possible, *get involved in supporting gifted education.* You can make an impact, not only for your child but for all children. We are all best served if all children are educated to achieve their full potential.

To effectively speak up for gifted kids, you'll need to position yourself to become an advocate rather than an adversary. An advocate is someone who pleads someone's case, and you'll get much better results if you think of yourself this way than if you think of yourself as going up against an enemy.

It's a fact of life that our society is sometimes biased against bright people. Society wants to make use of their gifts, but it doesn't want to make the investment in nurturing them. Teachers and administrators who support gifted education are a minority in their profession. Legislators and other decision-makers are generally not knowledgeable about gifted education issues. Federal spending is woefully lacking (only two cents of every hundred dollars for K–12 education is spent on gifted education), in part because of the commonly held myth that gifted students have no special educational needs. Parents must become advocates if gifted students are to get appropriate educational services, since we have the wisdom and knowledge it takes to fight for our children.

Six Steps to Advocacy

Whether you're advocating for your child within the classroom or for gifted children nationally, advocacy involves six simple steps:

1. **Gather information.** Knowledge is power. Know what your child needs, what services the schools can offer, and what strategies work well for gifted kids. Find out what problems and obstacles may stand in the way of achieving your goals.

2. **Identify allies.** Who are the people and organizations that share a common interest in improving gifted education? Connect with these people to have a greater impact.

3. **Learn the rules of the game.** Understand the process of how schools, school boards, education agencies, and law-makers decide on policy, regulation, and laws. To effect change, you'll need to understand how the system works.

4. **Keep written records.** Keep written records of meetings with teachers or other school personnel, the results of educational evaluations and assessments, samples of your child's work, and letters you send to policymakers.

5. **Propose solutions.** Identifying problems is easy. Discovering solutions is more difficult. As an advocate, you can help by suggesting specific, realistic solutions to improve gifted education.

6. **Be persistent.** Change doesn't happen overnight. The persistent dedication of parents and other community members can be a force for incremental change.

Begin close to home. First of all, keep informed about what's going on in your child's school. Become as active at the school or in the PTA as you possibly can, since this is a good way to learn what's happening both inside and outside the classroom. Help in your child's classroom whenever you can, and offer to share one of your talents or hobbies with the class. Get to know your child's teacher.

Listen to your child. When I would ask what my child did in school, the usual response was "Nothing." But I wanted to know what new information my child was learning, to ensure that there was some struggle with difficult concepts, not just a repetition of the same old information. Rather than asking, "What did you do in school today?" I learned to say instead, "What did you learn that was new to you?" or "What did you have to struggle to learn today?"

Don't hesitate to question everything you're told about gifted education. Surprisingly, not everything that's labeled gifted *is* gifted—or for that matter, even educationally sound. By becoming active, you'll be a terrific role model for your child. Your actions really do speak louder than words.

Getting Support for Yourself

As the parent of a gifted child, you may often feel stranded and alone. You are not alone! There are more than 2.5 *million* children in the United States alone who could be classified as gifted. They all have parents whose concerns and fears and hopes are likely similar to yours. All you have to do is find a few. Reach out and make some connections.

You'll get a lot out of joining a parent support group. Such groups offer moral support and companionship. Make sure the group has a purpose or mission. Look for a group that welcomes new members and does not charge an excessive fee. They may offer the chance to exchange ideas and increase your knowledge. Some groups sponsor speakers or programs on topics of interest. You may find other adults who will join with you in advocating for your kids.

If your school district doesn't have a support group for parents of gifted students, start one. Contact the gifted program coordinator for help. He or she may be able to put you in contact with other parents of gifted students. If your district doesn't have a gifted program coordinator, ask a teacher or principal for help in finding other parents of gifted and talented youngsters. You can also connect with parent groups in neighboring cities to find out how they got started, what problems they've encountered, what types of programs they have, and how they're supported (funds are needed for mailings, copying, refreshments, etc.).

If you are starting a support group, begin by finding a place to hold a meeting and set the time. You can post a notice at your local library, and be sure to talk to the children's librarian who may know some parents who might be interested in your group. Request to post an announcement in your school's newsletter. Contact your local newspaper in plenty of time to get a listing for the meeting. Set an agenda. Stay focused on your goal of providing for the needs of gifted students.

You may want to contact your state's affiliate of the National Association for Gifted Children. Most affiliates offer individual memberships. These groups are focused on meeting the needs of gifted children within the state. State conferences are normally held yearly and provide an excellent opportunity to find out new information, network, share ideas, and collaborate.

Gifted Advocacy Groups

These national organizations are good sources of information about giftedness. They provide a variety of services including journals, conventions, and networking opportunities. Although these are primarily professional organizations—for educators, researchers, counselors, etc.—parents can benefit, too.

The Council for Exceptional Children
1110 N. Glebe Road, Suite 300
Arlington, VA 22201
(703) 620-3660
www.cec.sped.org

Gifted Child Society
190 Rock Road
Glen Rock, NJ 07452
(201) 444-6530
www.gifted.org

National Association for Gifted Children
1707 L Street NW, Suite 550
Washington, DC 20036
(202) 785-4268
www.nagc.org

Gifted Canada
www3.telus.net/giftedcanada
This Web site offers links to provincial gifted organizations.

Assess the needs of other parents of gifted children. What issues are important to them? You can do this formally through a school questionnaire (be sure to get the school's okay first), or informally by phone. Once you've compiled a list of the other parents' needs, you can set some guidelines for prospective programs.

Having a clear agenda with a focus or topic can prevent meetings from turning into brag sessions or a series of "ain't it awful" tales. Topics can include parent concerns involving discipline, sibling rivalry, time management, program advocacy, and more. Think about inviting speakers, such as professionals who have knowledge of gifted children, staff from a local university, or even a panel of gifted kids.

Be sure to allow time for just plain conversation. Parents of gifted kids have often experienced the same or similar problems and many are willing to share solutions or hindsight with the group.

Try not to let it bother you if people outside the group suggest that you and the other parents are on an ego trip. In my experience, the reverse is most often true. If anything, most parents try to play down their childrens' giftedness, and some actually go so far as to deny it.

Like other parents of bright kids, you might have to make choices that aren't popular with relatives, neighbors, or friends who may disapprove if you attend school board meetings or decide to change schools, bus your child to a faraway school, educate her at home, or have her skip a grade. It's especially hard to stand up for your child when the disapproving voices are close and dear. At times like these, the support of a parent group or the empathy of another parent who understands can make all the difference in the world.

Advocacy on the Local Level

As a parent, you're part of the single largest power-wielding group in the school system, a group more powerful than teachers or administrators. Our schools are a reflection of our society, and you are a vital part of that society.

Without parent advocacy and participation, our gifted programs wouldn't survive. More than half of the gifted programs within local districts exist because of gifted kids' parents. Moms and dads working in a cooperative way with teachers, administrators, and school boards have successfully brought about major changes in their children's school settings.

Dorothy Knopper is an excellent example of such parent advocacy. Along with a small group of parents, Dorothy pushed for individualized education and a special curriculum for the gifted and talented. The group was instrumental in developing the exemplary gifted program that is in place today in Livonia, Michigan. On the state level, Dorothy's advocacy led to the Michigan legislation funding gifted education in 1974, as well as the hiring of a state consultant for the gifted.

Any time you put into improving the system is bound to benefit your child. So let's get started on the nuts and bolts of what you can do.

How to Be Heard: Begin with the Teacher

For a gifted program to be successful, everyone must cooperate and be willing to compromise a little. If your child's gifted program turns out not to be truly different from the regular program, or if the teacher simply isn't effective at providing gifted programming, you need to speak up for your child.

It helps to know your school district's philosophy statement on gifted education. Nearly all school districts have such a statement, and once you're familiar with it, you can use it as ammunition in your efforts to get your child's school to implement better programming. A typical philosophy statement might say: "All District 000 students are entitled to an education that is appropriate to their learning needs. . . . The District recognizes that a portion of our school population includes academically talented students. Such students benefit from differentiated educational programs. Programs for the academically talented will provide enrichment which is developmentally appropriate."

Other philosophy statements are more specific: "School district 111 believes that academically gifted students should be given the opportunity to maximize their potential in order to contribute to society and to attain personal fulfillment. The focus of this program is to develop higher levels of thinking skills, strategies for independent problem solving, and appropriate self-concept and self-esteem. This will be accomplished by compacting and accelerating in math with enrichment activities in the other academic areas. The classroom teacher in the regular classroom will provide the program with support materials supplied by the gifted facilitator."

Once you have the school's philosophy statement in hand, you can ask how this statement is becoming a reality for your child. You have the right and the responsibility to ask questions about how the philosophy is implemented. What is happening to assure that gifted students are given the opportunities envisioned? Has the gifted program been evaluated to assure that this is indeed happening? Does the school offer a program on paper only, or is it actually taking place? At what grade levels? How much funding is allocated for it to occur?

School systems are highly structured organizations. When you encounter a problem, it's generally best to start at the bottom and work your way to the top. Let's say you see a problem with your child's homework—he's being given too much repetition of material he already knows how to do. If he can master a particular concept in five problems, but the assignment is to do fifty, or if he's supposed to write his spelling words twenty times even though he already knows the list, it's time for you to communicate with your child's teacher.

If your child is having difficulty with a teacher, start with that teacher, not the principal or superintendent! If you contact someone higher up, the first question he or she will ask is if you've spoken with the teacher. Even if you think you know what the teacher's response will be, go there first. If you don't feel satisfied, then go to the principal—but never before trying the teacher.

Some school districts have coordinators of gifted services. Although they usually have heavy workloads and little free time, they may be friendly to your cause. Gifted coordinators understand the overall programming for the district and the needs of gifted and talented students. They also may have some powers of persuasion.

If your district hasn't specifically designated a program coordinator for gifted education, the director of special education may be your best source of information. Subject area or curriculum coordinators may provide additional help. If you can find an advocate within the system, you're more likely to be listened to than if you speak up alone.

Other parents with knowledge of the system and its workings can also be an asset. Your school district may have a gifted students' parent group, which can provide help and support. If there isn't one in your district, your state's gifted affiliate organization may know of a parent group nearby. Be as informed as possible about the school system, its resources, and its philosophy.

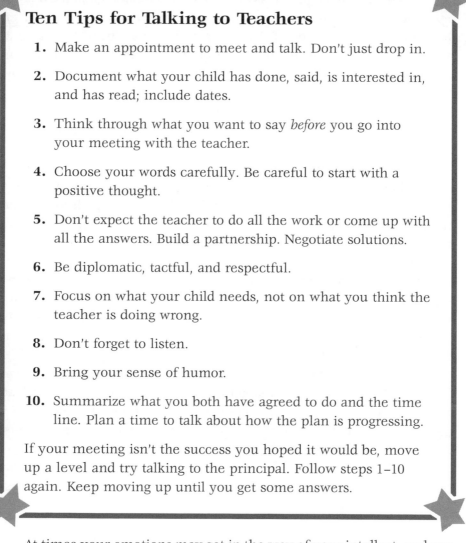

Ten Tips for Talking to Teachers

1. Make an appointment to meet and talk. Don't just drop in.

2. Document what your child has done, said, is interested in, and has read; include dates.

3. Think through what you want to say *before* you go into your meeting with the teacher.

4. Choose your words carefully. Be careful to start with a positive thought.

5. Don't expect the teacher to do all the work or come up with all the answers. Build a partnership. Negotiate solutions.

6. Be diplomatic, tactful, and respectful.

7. Focus on what your child needs, not on what you think the teacher is doing wrong.

8. Don't forget to listen.

9. Bring your sense of humor.

10. Summarize what you both have agreed to do and the time line. Plan a time to talk about how the plan is progressing.

If your meeting isn't the success you hoped it would be, move up a level and try talking to the principal. Follow steps 1–10 again. Keep moving up until you get some answers.

At times your emotions may get in the way of your intellect, and you may be tempted to strike out in inappropriate ways. Your impatience with the system may be justified, but tact is the key to getting your ideas heard and accepted. Be assertive, not aggressive.

Pushy, obnoxious parents often do more harm than good. If you're outraged about something that has happened, give yourself some time to cool off. Write your thoughts down, and keep them to yourself. Take a walk, burn off the excess energy, sleep on it. You want support, which you won't get if you alienate those with the power to bring about change.

One parent decided to give a gift to her child's teacher each year. She paid for her child's teacher to attend the state gifted education convention. She felt that the speakers her child's teacher heard and the resources available could improve the education of all students in the class—and especially the gifted kids. (If you decide to do this, check with the district first to make sure substitute teachers are available.) The parent organization could also make a similar gesture.

If you *demand* gifted classes, you'll meet resistance. You'll get further by saying something like, "I know you're doing an excellent job in your classroom (school, school system). It must be very difficult to meet all the different needs and abilities of every student. You're trying to do all you can. But there's one thing you can't give your gifted and talented students, even if you're the best teacher (administrator, school board), and that's the opportunity for them to be together, to network and share ideas. They need that opportunity, and that's why they must leave your class, or have different work within your class, at least for some of the time."

When it comes to talking to teachers—or anyone else you approach for help for your child—a little diplomacy goes a long way. Here are some examples of styles to try (and to avoid):

Instead of this:	**Try saying this:**
"Why don't you have a gifted program in place? What's wrong with this school?"	"I know the gifted program is new and you need time to develop the curriculum, but what will be done this year? How can I help?"
"Why aren't you providing _____ for the gifted kids in our district?"	"I can tell you want to be on the cutting edge. For that reason, I thought you'd like to know about (an article I've read; a new idea; a resource person; state and national gifted conferences . . .)."

continued

Instead of this:	Try saying this:
"Don't you know that this curriculum is outdated and inappropriate for my child?"	"How do you, the teacher (principal, superintendent, board member) feel about the district's curriculum? If you could make some changes, what would they be? Have you ever thought of _____?"

Working with the School Board

In many ways, schools are like a business, yet people with little expertise in that particular business essentially run them: school board members. School boards have the ultimate responsibility for decisions that involve the overall curriculum, staff, and expenditures within each school district.

School board members are elected representatives of the community dedicated to community service. Their time commitment is mammoth and admirable—with no pay, little recognition, and sometimes a lot of grief. They have been elected because they're concerned. But they are also individuals with favorite causes and gaps in their knowledge.

One group of parents who were unhappy that their school district ignored the needs of gifted students worked together for change. They felt their school district's philosophy stating that all children had the right to learn included gifted students in the all. When the school board resisted gifted programming, they formed a committee to search the community for potential school board candidates who supported gifted education. With the support and community involvement of these parents, the school board candidates they backed ran and were elected. With the majority of the school board members behind the gifted program, it had the necessary backbone and funding for success.

In working with school boards, it's helpful to know the members' backgrounds and to be aware of their individual strengths and weaknesses. Chat with board members over a cup of coffee. Provide articles or research briefs that support gifted education. Campaign for board members who hold ideals similar to yours and who speak up for gifted kids.

Attending a school board meeting can help you get to know board members and their interests. Make it a point to know what's going on, and learn to ask appropriate questions. Seek out board members who can be swayed to your perspective, and do whatever you can to win them over to your side. At the same time, find out who might oppose your cause. Talk with them, too. Hear their arguments and ask if they'll listen to yours. See if you can't find something to agree on, or a point where you're willing to compromise. The point isn't to argue, but to understand how others see the issue. Don't waste valuable time and energy in arguments that only build hostility. Offer to serve on a fact-finding committee or task force. Provide articles and research to support your case.

Getting "Them" Moving

In most cases, local school districts cannot provide adequate gifted programming without state funds. In the vast majority of states, parents, parent groups, and associations are involved in advocacy for gifted education. To get involved yourself—or better yet, with a group of other parents of gifted kids—start by finding out who in your area is eligible to receive state money and under what conditions. Any existing parent support group in your state can help you locate this information. Become familiar with your state's laws, rules, and regulations so that you know what is and isn't allowed.

In some states, local districts compete for state grants. In others, money is given to schools that identify gifted pupils as prescribed by law. Other variations exist as well. Find out how funding is distributed in your state, including when the funding becomes available and how long it lasts. Find out when decisions are made concerning funding and what other districts of similar size and population do.

Legislators—who can often be swayed by phone calls, letters, and meetings—vote on state gifted funds. Get to know your legislators, especially those on the K–12 education committees. You can offer to meet with your legislators when they are in their home offices. Don't be disappointed if you meet with an aide. Aides play a key role in developing and supporting legislation.

When meeting with a legislator or staff person, introduce yourself and the other advocates with you. Be sure to explain why you are there. Be concise. Review your points in ten minutes or less, and support your viewpoint with clear and concise written material that summarizes your points. Thank the legislator for the chance to present your information. Follow up with a thank-you note and a review of what you discussed. Be sure to respond to any requests that the legislator may have had. Stay in touch. Request that you be on the legislator's mailing list for any educational issues.

There is strength in numbers. Because legislators are elected, they may decide how to vote on an issue based on what they hear from their constituents. It is imperative, then, that you urge others who share your views to contact their legislators. Demonstrable public support enhances the chances of passing effective legislation. Don't leave students out of the process either. They can write letters to explain the benefits of gifted programming. Connect with state gifted organizations and talk to influential members of your community to get their support. They may have connections to legislators. Invite your legislator to visit your district's gifted program or state gifted convention. Use the local media to inform others. Take every opportunity to share information about gifted education issues.

It's important to understand how the legislative process works in order to be an effective advocate. Legislators write and introduce bills, but parents can educate legislators about the needs of gifted students so that bills addressing those needs stand a better chance of being introduced and passed. Here's an overview of the federal legislative process for education bills, which includes gifted education.* States generally use a similar process. (Your state representative can give you specific information on your state's process.)

1. The bill is introduced in the House or the Senate. Any senator or representative may introduce a bill at any time during the legislative session. The person who introduces the legislation is known as the sponsor. Any number of representatives or senators may cosponsor a bill. Bills are identified by number and numbered sequentially from the first day of the new Congress. Senate bills begin with S. House bills begin with H.R.

2. The numbered bill is referred to the appropriate committee for review (in this case, most likely the education committee). Legislative committees have office space and professional staff to assist with the administrative details and responsibilities involved in the consideration of bills.

3. Committees consider the proposed bill and provide a forum for the public to speak. They seek input from relevant federal departments and agencies. A committee may request a report from the Congressional Budget Office to get information on the costs associated with the bill or the General Accounting Office about the scope and size of the federal program the bill would change.

4. Public hearings are announced at least one week in advance. The committee chair introduces the bill and then senators or representatives who wish to be heard can testify. Cabinet officers, government officials, and interested private individuals can testify either voluntarily or by subpoena. Witnesses who appear are required to file a written statement in advance of their appearance and limit their presentations to a summary of their arguments. Complete written transcripts are printed and distributed by the committee.

*Adapted with permission from *Advancing Gifted and Talented Education in the Congress: An Advocacy Guide for Parents and Teachers* by National Association for Gifted Children, 1707 L Street NW, Suite 550, Washington, DC 20036, (202) 785-4268, *www.nagc.org.*

5. After the hearings are finished, the bill is marked up. A subcommittee considers the bill and then votes on what action to take. The bill may be reported favorably, unfavorably, or without recommendation. It can also be tabled, or postponed indefinitely. Each member of the subcommittee has one vote. This process is repeated in the full committee.

6. If the committee votes to report the bill to the House or Senate, the committee staff will write the committee report, which describes the purpose and scope of the bill and the reasons for its recommended approval. The report is filed with the House or Senate and assigned a report number. It is placed on the House or Senate calendar and waits for further action. The majority leadership determines how and when the bill will be considered on the floor.

7. Floor consideration differs in the House and Senate. After debate and approval of any amendments, legislators vote whether or not to pass the bill in its final form.

8. After a bill passes in one chamber, it is sent for consideration by the other. There, legislators may either hold a vote on the bill as it was received or refer it to the appropriate committee for deliberation. If the House and the Senate each pass a different version of the bill, a conference committee is appointed to iron out differences between the two versions of a bill. Both bodies must pass a bill in the same form before it can be presented to the President for signature to become law. A conference report of the committee explains the compromises. At this point, it cannot be amended and must be either accepted or rejected by the House and Senate as written.

9. If the bill is approved by both the House and Senate, the bill is enrolled for presentation to the President.

10. The bill becomes law if the President signs the bill or if the President does not return the bill with objections to Congress within ten days of receiving it. If the President vetoes the bill, it can still become law if two-thirds of both the House and Senate vote to override the veto.

There are many places in this process where gifted legislation and funding can be increased, decreased, or totally cut. Your state's legislative process is likely similar. Check with your state legislators to find out about current legislation and funding that could affect your district.

How's Your State Doing?

When the Council of State Directors of Programs for the Gifted took a nationwide survey in 1998–99, it found that twenty-six states have laws or rules mandating services for gifted education. Seventeen states have laws mandating programming. Delaware didn't have a mandate for services, but it had gifted programs in all of its school districts anyway. Some states mandate identification and services for gifted students but do not appropriate specific funds for them. Funding for gifted programs is the key issue.

States also vary in how they identify students to receive gifted programming. Some require individual intelligence test scores, while many other states merely recommend using them. A few states require teacher certification, and a much greater number recommend it. Several states review the past products and accomplishments of students when considering whether they fit the definition of gifted and talented.

The 1998–1999 State of the States Gifted and Talented Education Report reported that the following had the greatest positive impact on gifted and talented education:

- improved identification procedures

- expanded professional development in gifted education

- increased accountability and better program monitoring, program effectiveness standards, and reporting methods

- increased funding for gifted education

- new state legislation supporting gifted education and improved regulation

- improved programming

- adoption of state assessments and state content standards

- designated gifted and talented staff at the state education agency

Not surprisingly, states also reported that the following had the greatest negative impact on gifted education:

- funding issues, including uneven funding from year to year, changes in funding methods, limited funding, or lack of funding

- education reform efforts that focus only on improving the achievement of low-performing students, high-stakes assessment programs, anti-grouping sentiment, inclusion, etc.

- lack of personnel at the state education agency responsible for gifted education

- lack of accountability, including nonexistent program standards

In addition to these, the survey also identified a few other areas that, if given attention, have the potential to improve gifted education considerably:

- advocacy efforts

- attention to early childhood gifted programming

- state and federal legislative support for gifted education

- improved state technical assistance to local school districts

Getting Your Message Across

So how do you get your message across to the people who can take action? Telephoning and writing letters to your legislators are the keys.

Your letters and phone calls can ensure that gifted education will be considered seriously, especially when they come at crucial points in the legislative process. The League of Women Voters or other organizations may be able to help you discover those times, as well as the names and contact information for your legislators.

If you are unsure who your Congress members are, there are easy ways to find out. Visit *www.congress.org* and enter your Zip code in the search box. The House of Representatives *(www.house.gov)* and the Senate *(www.senate.gov)* both have Web sites that list members of Congress, or you can call the Capitol operator at (202) 224-3121 and ask to be connected to legislators.

continued

Your local office of the League of Women Voters can also help. Visit the national Web site at *www.lwv.org* or check your local phone book for more information.

Telephoning a legislator works best when the message is simply "I urge you to vote for X" or "Support XYZ." A written letter is the most effective means of explaining why the support is needed. Email may seem easy, but with the proliferation of spam and the sheer volume of email legislators receive, paper letters may actually get through faster and are certainly more highly respected.

The following pages contain samples you can use to start writing letters. Keep the following guidelines in mind:

- Use personal or business letterhead when possible.

- Refer to a bill number if writing about specific legislation.

- Give your reason for writing. When representing a group, include that information. Use personal stories—they make strong supporting arguments.

- Be constructive. Offer alternatives if you oppose a measure.

- Ask the legislator to state his or her position in a written reply.

- Thank your legislator for support. Compliment when you can.

Form for Letter to Legislator

Date

The Honorable Representative/Senator
State Capitol Building   or   United States House of
                                        Representatives/Senate
City, State, ZIP   or   Washington, DC 20515/20510

continued

Dear Representative/Senator:

Inform the legislator that:

- You are a voting member of his or her district.

- You are concerned about gifted education in your legislative district.

Elaborate on the program your child participates in.

Tell the legislator what you want from him or her. For example:

- "I would like you to vote (for/against) House Bill (give the exact number of that year's bill)" or "I urge you to support the educational needs of gifted students by cosponsoring bill number . . ."

- Be specific about the action you'd like, including the amount of funding.

Finally, ask the legislator to send you a written reply to your letter, informing you of how he or she feels about the issue, and how he or she will vote.

Sample Letter to Legislator

April 20, 2002

The Honorable Senator Bigbill
State Capitol Building
Springfield, IL 62706

Dear Senator Bigbill:

I am very concerned about gifted education in Legislative District 41. As a registered voter, I appreciated your vote for Senate Bill 3065 last year. My local school, Mighty Elementary, has an excellent gifted program, which my son John enjoys

continued

very much. This program has helped him excel in math. The regular classroom curriculum did not challenge his abilities, but through the gifted program, his teachers accelerated his study of math and helped him learn to think like a mathematician. His need for advanced programming was met and his love of math expanded.

I am writing you regarding HB 494, which includes funding for gifted education (between lines 22 and 29). Many of the parents at Mighty Elementary are concerned that the program and our children's education will decline without the state appropriation to our local district. Increasing the amount of funding for gifted students to $100 per child would make great strides in providing the services these children need to succeed. This increase to $7.86 million on line 24 of the bill would greatly assist our local district with supplies and materials vital to the gifted program.

Would you please write to me, giving your views on funding for gifted education and telling me how you intend to vote on HB 494?

Sincerely yours,

Sample Phone Call Script

Hello, my name is _____. I'm a registered voter in Senator/Representative _____'s district, and my child attends _____ school in the district. I'm concerned about gifted education legislation and want to know the Senator's/ Reprentative's views. I feel that the bill should increase the amount of funding for gifted students to $_____. This

continued

increase would greatly assist our local district with supplies and materials vital to the gifted program.

I would appreciate a personal letter from Senator/Representative _____ informing me how he/she intends to vote on Bill # _____.

My name is spelled _____, and my address is _____. I'd appreciate hearing from the Senator/Representative prior to the vote on this bill.

Thank you.

Receptionists handle the bulk of the calls to congressional offices. Sometimes it is possible to speak with a staff member assigned to your issue. When making a phone call:

- State your view clearly and succinctly. Time is precious.

- Request action.

- Leave your name, address, and phone number.

Email

Email messages can be the least effective means of getting your message across. Congressional offices are deluged with so much email that staff members may not take the time to read and respond personally to each message. Because email doesn't come on letterhead, messages that should carry weight, like those from statewide gifted education associations, aren't as easily distinguished from others. Letters on letterhead carry much more weight than email. Email can be an effective way to communicate with staff, but they are less effective for elected officials.

A Few Final Words

It's not easy to raise *any* child, much less a curious, creative, intense, gifted, and talented child. But if you do your best to see that your child gets an excellent education, and if you hold on to your sense of humor while all about you are losing theirs, you *will* survive these challenging years. And your payoff will be one great, interesting adult. Good luck!

Learn More About It

Advancing Gifted and Talented Education in Congress: An Advocacy Guide for Parents and Teachers 2000 (Washington, DC: National Association for Gifted Children, 2000). A concise and powerful course in federal advocacy that makes advocacy fun.

Advocacy in Action: An Advocacy Handbook for Gifted and Talented Education by the California Association for the Gifted (Whittier, CA: California Association for the Gifted, 1998). Practical planning and how to speak up for your child.

Parent Education: Parents as Partners by Dorothy Knopper (Boulder, CO: Open Space Communications, 1997). Clearly written, easy-to-understand ways for parents to collaborate with schools.

Stand Up for Your Gifted Child by Joan Franklin Smutny (Minneapolis: Free Spirit Publishing, 2001). A practical resource on advocacy that promotes collaboration between home and school.

15 Questions Parents Ask— and 14½ Answers

Some questions don't have answers,
which is a terribly difficult lesson to learn.
—Katherine Graham

1. What can I do if my child is an underachiever?

When you expect more from your child than you're getting, whatever his IQ, you're likely to perceive him as an "underachiever." This is actually a rather subjective label—meaning it's a matter of opinion.

One thing to consider is whether you're constantly pushing him to do more than he's comfortable doing. If he feels he can't possibly live up to your goals for him no matter how hard he tries, he may simply stop trying. *Voilà*—an underachiever.

Some gifted kids resolve conflicts within themselves by mentally "dropping out." For example, if they want very much to be popular, they may hide their giftedness. This can happen if their peer group makes it clear that it's not cool to always get the best grades and come up with the right answers.

Some kids find that underachieving can also be a good (but passive) way to get even with parents, especially near the teen years. "I know that ever since I was born, Dad has expected me to go to an Ivy League college and follow in his footsteps and be a lawyer. But I don't want to play the game," explains one young man. "I'm tired of the pressure." Counseling might help a family like this to confront some of their deeper issues.

I know a teenage girl who began underachieving so early that she never had a chance to be identified as gifted. Whenever she felt that any-one was getting close to her giftedness, she covered it up. There wasn't ever any doubt that she could do the work. She was able to ace advanced math after a few weeks in a summer course after goofing off all during her senior year in high school. But she was mainly interested in being well liked, and it wasn't popular to be gifted. Even counseling didn't help her, because when a child decides to dig in her heels, there isn't a lot that can be done about it. Kids ultimately have to make their own choices.

One thing you can do, especially with a creative underachiever, is to work with your child on developing organizational skills. Help him strike a balance between being creative and being organized. Some super-creative types seem to think that being organized and sticking to a project until it's finished will take something away from their creativity. Show that it won't by modeling follow-through behavior on a creative project of your own.

2.   What kinds of activities are best for my child at home?

You can apply some of what we've learned about good gifted programs to your child's everyday activities. For example, in order to help your child develop higher-level thinking skills, you might ask her to compare and contrast two stories or two different versions of the same story. Or read a story and leave the ending unfinished so she can complete it. Your child can practice evaluation by determining which story she likes better.

Even the hours spent watching TV can be educational if you encourage higher-level thinking instead of passive watching. For example, ask your child to compare and contrast two different programs, create a different ending to a program, or evaluate the worth of a particular program, series, or performance.

Suggest that your child group or classify her collections in different ways. Encourage her to think up different uses for household objects or new inventions to solve old problems (a better mousetrap?).

Even young children should be allowed to choose between wearing the red sweater or the blue one. Be sure to ask why your child made a particular choice. Her reasons may enlighten you and prove thought-provoking for her.

Share your hobbies and interests with your child. Share the wonder of the world in the form of books, trips, and people. Look for historical points of interest, rocks, wiggly things, and new plant life. Discuss ideas.

Activities like cooking offer excellent opportunities for learning at home. The process includes reading and talking about the recipe, following the recipe, examining the ingredients, looking at how each is important, and, if one of the ingredients is missing, deciding what could be substituted and how this would change the recipe. Then you get to taste your creation. Suggested questions: Do you think this is a good recipe? Why? How could it be improved? What's your favorite food? Why?

3. My daughter is always saying she's bored at school. How can I tell if the work is inappropriate or if she's just lazy?
A lot of kids say their schoolwork is boring. Your daughter's work may really be boring and unchallenging, or she may be using this line as an excuse for not doing her homework or not performing up to her potential.

Start by talking to her teacher. Try to find out if the work is too easy, repetitive, or generally uninteresting. It's not likely that laziness is the problem, but maybe your daughter needs to learn some strategies for dealing with boredom.

I remember one kindergartner who always said, "I'm bored." I said to him, "I don't understand, there's all this stuff to do. What does *bored* mean to you?" He responded, "It means having to do what you want me to do rather than what I want to do." In other words, he was trying to get out of work that was assigned.

We need to explain that life is not always fun. Everyone gets bored at times, and there are things we have to do that we don't want to do.

If your daughter complains about being bored when she's stuck waiting somewhere, you might teach her to fool around with mind games or puns or something else to keep her mind busy.

4. My very bright boy wants to read all the time. What should I do?
Let him read a great deal of the time when he wants to, but also introduce him to the joys of going for a walk, playing a game, and playing with others. If you overreact or seem too worried or alarmed, you may force him into more of the same behavior. On the other hand, he needs to maintain a balance of physical and mental activity to stay healthy and to have a well-rounded life.

5. My very bright boy never wants to do anything but work at the computer. What should I do?
Get him books and magazines about subjects he likes. Make time to go for a walk and talk about his interests. Plan outings. Enjoy physical activity together. Going overboard on anything is not good. Be sure to monitor what he is doing on the computer and with whom he is communicating. Computers are both wonderful and horrid, depending on their use.

6. I think—no, I'm sure—that my child is smarter than I am. Is there anything special I need to know or do?

Although your child may have a higher IQ than you do, you've lived longer and have more wisdom. You need to be the one who's in control.

Don't be intimidated by your child's IQ, even if it's astronomical. If your child is interested in nuclear physics, you may never be able to keep up with what she learns. But there are other things she needs to know that you must help her with, such as tact, manners, and social acceptance. Perhaps you can share with her one of your hobbies or passions, whether it's singing or stamp collecting. Meanwhile, don't underestimate your own abilities. You'll always have something to teach your child. You have lived longer and have wisdom of advanced years to share.

7. One of my sons is gifted, the other isn't. Now what?

When two of my children were tested for giftedness during kindergarten, and one was identified for the gifted program and the other wasn't, I chose not to have the first child placed in the gifted program because I didn't want one labeled and one not. Instead, I enrolled them both at an arts alternative magnet school. This solution catered to their creative bent and avoided the "one is, one isn't" problem.

Not long ago, identical eleven-year-old twins applied to a New York City junior high school for the gifted and talented—and only one was accepted. Their grades were identical, but one girl was more talented in drama than the other. Their parents vowed to fight the decision. The headline of the article in *USA Today* read, "Life's not fair, NYC twins learn."

You can help make life more "fair" for your kids by recognizing each child's uniqueness, which has nothing to do with IQ scores. Accentuate the specialness of each one. Since your gifted child is probably already getting special attention because of his giftedness, and is perhaps attending special classes, look for something his sibling excels at or is interested in, and take *him* for classes, too.

One caution: If you have a slow child and a gifted child, and you're always giving extra attention to the slow child to help him catch up, the gifted one may play down his gifts in order to get equal time from you. Make the effort to focus on your gifted child so he doesn't feel slighted.

8. How soon should my daughter's school test her for giftedness?

Some school districts now test as early as preschool. A few states mandate gifted programming for kindergarten through twelfth grade. Check into what's required in your state and what's available in your own district. If you suspect that your child is a gifted preschooler, but her teacher doesn't seem to notice anything special about her, share your observations and feelings with the teacher.

9. How can I get my son to understand why "process" is important? He insists on putting only the answers down on his math papers, since it's so easy for him to figure out word problems in his head. He won't show his steps, even though the teacher demands it. And this affects his grades.

Try explaining to him that knowing *how* to do something is just as important as coming up with the right answer. Once he learns the steps necessary to figure out the answers to his word problems, he'll be better equipped for more advanced mathematical calculations.

Sometimes kids are graded down when they make mistakes during the computation stage, even though their final answers are correct. This may not seem fair to them, but it's important to show the process so the teacher can see their mistakes. If they consistently make errors in addition or multiplication, eventually they won't arrive at the right answers, once the problems get too complicated to do mentally.

10. Ever since my daughter entered puberty, she doesn't want to share any part of her social life with me. She used to tell me everything. How can I get back in touch with her?

What you're describing is the most natural process in the world. It's all part of your child's need to separate from you so she can become a fully independent adult.

Somewhere around puberty, when those devil hormones kick in, children decide that confiding in peers is safer and more fun than telling their parents all the fascinating details of their lives. Psychologists advise you to stay cool, keep sharing parts of your own life (if your child is interested), resist the temptation to pressure your child for information (or you'll get the opposite results from what you want), and don't take her need for privacy personally—it really doesn't have anything to do with you.

Be especially careful not to criticize when she does leak a detail or two about her life. And don't keep pushing for more and more on those rare occasions when she opens up a little. Just be a good listener. Many teenagers complain that their parents never listen to them when they do talk, so they no longer bother to talk. And be patient: If she used to tell you everything, one of these days, when the tumult of adolescence is past, she'll once again tell you *some* things.

11. Which is better for my gifted child—public school, private school, or homeschooling?

It depends on your child's needs, your family's values, your financial situation and willingness to sacrifice, how good the schools in your area are—both public and private—and how capable and comfortable you feel about educating your child. And it depends on how good the gifted program is (or whether one exists) at the particular school you're considering.

You'll need to do some investigating. Visit every school you might consider for your child and ask a lot of questions. Ask everyone you know to share with you what he or she knows about the schools their kids attend, but don't accept what someone else says without checking it out yourself.

If your local public school has a responsive principal, an intelligently run gifted program, and caring teachers, there are many advantages to sending your child there. If, however, you don't get a good feeling about any of these areas when you visit, you and your child might be happier at a private school. But only if it's a private school that has a responsive headmaster, creative programs that allow gifted kids to do some independent learning, and teachers who care about—and understand—bright children.

More and more parents are choosing to homeschool their children. This requires a huge commitment of time and resources. By homeschooling, you can teach according to your child's learning style and preferred intelligences. You can tailor the curriculum specifically for your child. The student can learn more material faster without waiting for others to catch up. For more on homeschooling, see pages 118–120.

12. How many after-school activities are too many for my child?

That depends on your child. One fourth-grader told me that he never wanted to take another extra class or lesson for as long as he lived. "But you're so good at everything," I pointed out. "That's just it," he answered. "Monday night's hockey, Tuesday night's swimming, Wednesday night's church, Thursday night's chess club. I have no time for myself!"

Scheduling your child's every waking moment fails to allow for self-directed time. Kids need to learn how to fill a free hour or two on their own without being "bored" or expecting to be entertained.

When my children were younger, I let them choose one outside activity for each grading period or semester. As the parent who had to get them from one activity to the next, I needed to recognize my own limits, too. Just because you have a bright kid doesn't mean you won't have to say, "I know that you're interested in all these activities, but I only have a certain amount of time and energy." Intense children are exhausting, and if you have more than one, they'll inevitably go in different directions.

13. What can I do about my obnoxious kid?

If by "obnoxious" you mean a "know-it-all" child who can't be told any-thing and has to have everything *her* way, it's time to take action! This is the kind of kid nobody wants to be around. She needs to learn how her behavior affects others. And she needs to become more sensitive to their needs, not just her own.

Sometimes it's difficult for these kids to hear, and your advice may be most noticeable if it's modeled. Show her what it's like to be on the receiving end of obnoxious or abrasive behavior. Say, "I'm going to show you what your behavior looks like. Then I want you to tell me how it feels to you." Give her an example and talk about it afterward.

Maybe your child's obnoxiousness is the result of ongoing power struggles between the two of you. If so, it's time for you to establish some good, fair, consistent rules—and stick to them no matter what. These will give your child a sense of security and a baseline for behavior, as well as the knowledge that someone older and wiser is in charge.

Generally speaking, a workable rule should:

- have a single interpretation. Agree on the details. For example, if you determine that everyone must be ready for school before breakfast, define what you mean by "ready."

- be realistic. Is the rule enforceable? Can your child really obey it? Do you break the rule yourself? Are you in a position to check to see that the rule is followed?

- be open to discussion with your child. She needs to see why the rule is needed and how she might benefit by it.

- have consequences if it's not followed. What can your child expect if she breaks the rule?

14. What about me? When is it my turn?

Just as most gifted kids feel insecure from time to time, so do their par-ents! At times it may seem as if you're treading uncharted waters, stranded and alone. That's when you need other parents of bright children from whom you can grab a lifeline. Your own family members may not be the ones to turn to, since they may not understand what you're going through with your challenging child.

Seek out support from the parents of your kids' gifted friends. Parents have told me, over and over, "It's so comforting to know that other parents have kids who have read every book in the library, and they don't know what to do with them either." It helps to hear from other parents whose children have experimented with the gas stove, or torn apart the mantle clock to see how it works, or trained their cat to sleep in the bathroom sink. Mostly, it helps to know that you're not alone.

Parents, like other professionals, experience burnout—it's just not as popular to admit it. Your social and emotional needs are important, too, and shouldn't be ignored. Here are some steps you can take to protect your own mental health:

- Have a life of your own. Develop your own hobbies and interests. Take pride in your work.

- Be careful not to overinvest in your child. Living for him and through him isn't good for either of you.

- Take time for your creative self. Find ways to express your thoughts and feelings. Look for things you enjoy doing—things that make you feel renewed.

- Replace stressful thoughts with calming ones. Concentrate on the positive. Appreciate the good things going on around you and the people you care about.

- Have adult friends. This may sound obvious, but with the time commitments that gifted kids require, some parents don't allow themselves time to be with their own friends. Find friends who inspire you and give you energy.

15. Am I doing everything right for my child?
That's a BIG question! Here's half of an answer: Only *you* know that for sure.

Hint: if you've read this far, you're a sincere, concerned parent who's *trying* to do everything right. Anyway, perfectionism is a no-no. Why not give yourself an A?

More Resources
for Parents

Alvino, James. "Considerations and Strategies for Parenting the Gifted Child." Storrs, CT: NRC/GT, 1995. Available online at *www.gifted.uconn.edu/alvino.html.* Brief practical suggestions for working with gifted children at home.

Birely, Marlene. *Crossover Children: A Sourcebook for Helping Children Who Are Gifted and Learning Disabled* (Reston, VA: Council for Exceptional Children, 1995). A helpful resource for parents of children who have dual exceptionalities.

Clark, Gilbert A., and Enid D. Zimmerman. *Educating Artistically Talented Students* (Syracuse, NY: Syracuse University Press, 1984). An excellent resource for looking at artistic talent.

——. *Resources for Educating Artistically Talented Students* (Syracuse, NY: Syracuse University Press, 1984). After schools have identified the artistically talented student, this book provides the resources necessary to educate them.

Cohen, LeoNora M., and E. Frydenberg. *Coping for Capable Kids: Strategies for Parents, Teachers, and Students* (Waco, TX: Prufrock Press, 1996). Designed to help gifted children, their parents, and teachers consider a variety of coping strategies for dealing with concerns; separated into two parts: one for teachers and parents, the other for preadolescents and adolescents.

Colangelo, Nicholas, and Davis, Gary A. *Handbook of Gifted Education* (Needham Heights, MA: Allyn & Bacon, 1996). A comprehensive handbook with support.

Davis, Gary A., and Sylvia B. Rimm. *Education of the Gifted and Talented* (Needham Heights, MA: Allyn & Bacon, 1997). An introductory textbook on gifted education.

Dinkmeyer, Don Sr., Gary D. McKay, and Don Dinkmeyer Jr. *The Parent's Handbook: Systematic Training for Effective Parenting (STEP)* (Circle Pines, MN: American Guidance Service, 1997). This handbook has helped many parents—the section on how to use active listening is extremely useful.

Ford, Donna Y. *Reversing Underachievement Among Gifted Black Students* (New York: Teachers College Press, 1996). This book explores what needs to be done to attack underachievement in gifted African-American students.

Ford, Donna Y., and J. John Harris III. *Multicultural Gifted Education* (New York: Teachers College Press, 1999). Guidelines for identifying and serving gifted students from multicultural populations.

Halsted, Judith Wynn. *Some of My Best Friends Are Books: Guiding Gifted Readers from Preschool to High School* (Scottsdale, AZ: Great Potential Press, 2002). More than three hundred books are listed that address the emotional and intellectual needs of gifted kids. Guided discussions are included with the annotated, summarized entries which are organized by age and topic.

Karnes, Frances A., and R.G. Marquardt. *Gifted Children and the Law: Mediation, Due Process and Court Cases* (Scottsdale, AZ: Great Potential Press, 1991). Compiles and analyzes legal actions related to identification and programming for gifted youth.

———. *Gifted Children and Legal Issues: An Update* (Scottsdale, AZ: Great Potential Press, 2000). Stories of parents who have had problems in obtaining an appropriate education for their gifted children and how they worked to resolve them.

Kerr, Barbara A. *Smart Girls* (Scottsdale, AZ: Great Potential Press, 1997). Helps parents, educators, and counselors understand gifted and talented girls. Biographies of eminent females and their experiences are included.

Kerr, Barbara A., and Sanford J. Cohn. *Smart Boys: Talent, Manhood, and the Search for Meaning* (Scottsdale, AZ: Great Potential Press, 2001). This book describes issues facing our brightest boys and men, and the concerns of those around them.

Piirto, Jane. *Talented Children and Adults: Their Development and Education* (Upper Saddle River, NJ: Prentice Hall, 1999). A comprehensive introduction to the characteristics and education of gifted individuals, focusing on factors that influence and encourage talent, from birth through adulthood.

———. *Understanding Those Who Create* (Scottsdale, AZ: Great Potential Press, 1998). A study of creativity with biographies of talented people.

Rimm, Sylvia B. *Why Bright Kids Get Poor Grades and What You Can Do About It* (New York: Crown Publishing, 1995). Describes how underachievement patterns can be a result of family interactions.

Smutny, Joan F,. ed. *The Young Gifted Child: Potential and Promise, an Anthology* (Cresskill, NJ: Hampton Press, 1998). A collection of articles by experts on the young gifted child.

Smutny, Joan F., Kathleen Veenker, and Stephen Veenker. *Your Gifted Child: How to Recognize and Develop the Special Talents in Your Child from Birth to Age Seven* (New York: Ballantine Books, 1994). A resource for parenting young gifted children.

Stone, Nancy. *Gifted Is Not a Dirty Word: Thoughts About Being Bright in an Average World* (Irvine, CA: Technicom, 1989). Tips on how to have a positive attitude about giftedness.

Strip, Carol, with Gretchen Hirsch. *Helping Gifted Children Soar: A Practical Guide for Parents and Teachers* (Scottsdale, AZ: Great Potential Press, 2000). A beginning book for parents and teachers who are starting to learn about gifted education. Also available in Spanish as *Ayudando a Niños Dotados a Volar.*

Tomlinson, Carol Ann. *The Differentiated Classroom: Responding to the Needs of All Learners* (Alexandria, VA: Association for Supervision and Curriculum Development, 1999). Presents methods to teachers for differentiating curriculum.

VonGruben, Jill F. *College Countdown: The Parent's and Student's Survival Kit for the College Admissions Process* (New York: McGraw Hill, 1999). This resource makes the intensive and enormous job of college planning achievable with minimal stress.

Webb, James T., and Arlene DeVries. *Gifted Parent Groups: The SENG Model* (Scottsdale, AZ: Great Potential Press, 1998). An effective model for establishing parent groups.

West, Thomas. *In the Mind's Eye: Visual Thinkers, Gifted People with Dyslexia and Other Learning Difficulties* (New York: Prometheus Books, 1997). A hopeful, fascinating study of gifted people with learning disabilities and visual-spatial strengths.

Winner, Ellen. *Gifted Children: Myths and Realities* (New York: Basic Books, 1997). Learn about the biological basis of giftedness, as well as the role played by parents and schools in nurturing exceptional abilities.

Periodicals

Gifted Child Today
Prufrock Press
P.O. Box 8813
Waco, TX 76714
1-800-998-2208
www.prufrock.com
A magazine full of ideas for educating talented learners.

Gifted Child Quarterly
National Association for Gifted Children (NAGC)
1707 L Street NW, Suite 550
Washington, D.C. 20036
(202) 785-4268
www.nagc.org
Recent research and developments in the field of gifted education. Available with NAGC membership.

Gifted Education Communicator: A Journal for Educators and Parents
California Association for the Gifted
1215 K Street, Suite 940
Sacramento, CA 95814
(916) 441-3999
www.cagifted.org
A quarterly publication for parents and educators of the gifted.

Parenting for High Potential
National Association for Gifted Children (NAGC)
1707 L Street NW, Suite 550
Washington, D.C. 20036
(202) 785-4268
www.nagc.org
Designed for parents, this quarterly magazine discusses issues gifted children face at home, in the community, and at school. Available with NAGC membership.

TEMPO
Texas Association for the Gifted and Talented
406 E. Eleventh Street, Suite 310
Austin, TX 78701
(512) 499-8248
www.txgifted.org
Quarterly journal focused on gifted education. Offers articles on a variety of themes and issues.

Understanding Our Gifted
Open Space Communications, Inc.
P.O. Box 18268
Boulder, CO 80308
1-800-494-6178
www.openspacecomm.com
For parents, educators, and counselors, this publication includes practical advice, social and emotional concerns, strategies for home and school, and educational options. Ten years of back issues are available.

Web Sites

American Association for Gifted Children at Duke University
www.aagc.org
The oldest gifted advocacy organization in the nation, it publishes educational materials for researchers, parents, and educators.

Davidson Institute for Talent Development
www.ditd.org
Helps parents, professionals, and students offer support for profoundly gifted young people.

Gifted-Children.com
www.gifted-children.com
An online parents' newsletter with networking opportunities and information on identifying and nurturing gifted children.

Gifted Child Society
www.gifted.org
A New Jersey–based nonprofit offers parents excerpts from the Gifted Child Society's newsletter, seminars, and a discussion forum where parents can share their experiences, concerns, and ideas.

Gifted Development Center, Denver
www.gifteddevelopment.com
Offers parents, schools, and advocacy groups information about identification, assessment, counseling, learning styles, programs, presentations, and resources for gifted children and adults.

GT World
www.gtworld.org
An online support community for parents of gifted children to explore topics such as parenting and advocating for children, teaching them how to advocate for themselves, obtaining an appropriate education, helping gifted kids with learning disabilities, and more.

Hoagies' Gifted Education Page
www.hoagiesgifted.org
Links to resources on nearly every aspect of gifted education available on the Internet, plus annotations and firsthand information provided by parents.

Hollingworth Center for Highly Gifted Children
www.hollingworth.org
A national support and resource network focused on the needs of highly gifted children.

National Foundation for Gifted and Creative Children
www.nfgcc.org
Information for parents about gifted and creative children.

National Research Center on the Gifted and Talented
www.gifted.uconn.edu/nrcgt.html
The National Research Center on the Gifted and Talented is sponsored by the U.S. Department of Education to investigate, develop, and disseminate new methods for identifying and teaching gifted students.

Supporting Emotional Needs of the Gifted
www.SENGifted.org
Information on identification, guidance, and effective ways to live and work with gifted children.

TAGFAM (Families of the Gifted and Talented)
www.tagfam.org
An international online organization serving families of intellectually gifted children.

World Council for Gifted and Talented Children
www.WorldGifted.ca
A global networking organization with an active membership of educators, scholars, researchers, parents, educational institutions, and others interested in giftedness.

Bibliography

Chapter 1

Council of State Directors of Programs for the Gifted. (1999). *The 1998–1999 State of the States Gifted and Talented Education Report.* Washington, DC: National Association for Gifted Children.

———. (2001). *State of the States Gifted and Talented Education Report, 1999–2000.* Washington, DC: National Association for Gifted Children.

Cox, June, Neil Daniel, and Bruce Boston. (1985). *Educating Able Learners: Programs and Promising Practices.* Austin, TX: University of Texas Press.

Delisle, James. (Spring 2001). "The 'G' Word (Shhh!)," *Understanding Our Gifted* 13 (3): 7–8.

Finn, Chester E., Jr., and Michael J. Petrilli, eds. (2000). *The State of State Standards 2000.* Washington, DC: The Thomas B. Fordham Foundation.

Galton, Francis. (1892). *Hereditary Genius.* London: Macmillan. Available online at *www.mugu.com/galton/index.html.*

Landrum, Mary, Carolyn Callahan, and Beverly Shaklee, eds. (2001). *Aiming for Excellence: Annotations to the NAGC Pre-K–Grade 12 Gifted Program Standards.* Washington, DC: National Association for Gifted Children.

Marland, S. (1972). *Education and the Gifted and Talented.* Washington, DC: Commission of Education.

Office of Educational Research and Improvement. (1993). *National Excellence: A Case for Developing America's Talent.* Washington, DC: U.S. Department of Education.

Ostwald, Peter. (1987). *Schumann: The Inner Voices of a Musical Genius.* Boston: Northeastern University Press.

Terman, Louis M. (1947). *Mental and Physical Traits of a Thousand Gifted Children,* vol. 1 of *Genetic Studies of Genius.* Stanford, CA: Stanford University Press.

Chapter 2

The American Association of University Women Educational Foundation. (1995). *The AAUW Report: How Schools Shortchange Girls.* New York: Marlowe and Company.

Badolato, Leigh A. (1998). "Recognizing and Meeting Special Needs of Gifted Females," *Gifted Child Today* November/December, 32–37.

Baum, S., S.V. Owen, and J. Dixon. (1991). *To Be Gifted and Learning Disabled: From Identification to Practical Intervention Strategies.* Mansfield Center, CT: Creative Learning Press.

Brody, L.E., and C.J. Mills. (1997). "Gifted Children with Learning Disabilities: A Review of the Issues," *Journal of Learning Disabilities* 30 (3): 282–286.

Burks, B.S., D.W. Jensen, and L. Terman. (1930). *Genetic Studies of Genius: Volume 3: The Promise of Youth: Follow-up Studies of a Thousand Gifted Children.* Stanford, CA: Stanford University Press.

Ciha, Thomas, Ruth Harris, Charlotte Hoffman, and Meredith Potter. (1974). "Parents as Identifiers of Giftedness, Ignored but Accurate," *Gifted Child Quarterly* Autumn, 191–195.

Clark, Barbara. (1997). *Growing Up Gifted.* Columbus, OH: Charles E. Merrill.

Cornell, D. (1989). "Child Adjustment and Parent Use of the Term 'Gifted,'" *Gifted Child Quarterly* 33 (2): 59–64.

Ellston, T. (1993). "Gifted and Learning Disabled: A Paradox?" *Gifted Child Today* 16 (1): 17–19.

Fox, L.H., L. Brody, and D. Tobin, (1983). *Learning Disabled/Gifted Children: Identification and Programming.* Austin, TX: PRO-ED, Inc.

Galbraith, Judy, and Jim Delisle. (1996). *The Gifted Kids' Survival Guide: A Teen Handbook.* Minneapolis: Free Spirit Publishing.

Gardner, Howard. (1984). *Frames of Mind: The Theory of Multiple Intelligences.* New York: Basic Books.

Jacobs, Jon. (1971). "Effectiveness of Teacher and Parent Identification of Gifted Children as a Function of School Level," *Psychology in the Schools* 8: 140–42.

Karnes, M.B., and L.J. Johnson. (1991). "Gifted Handicapped." In *Handbook of Gifted Education,* 1st ed., edited by N. Colangelo and G.A. Davis. Needham Heights, MA: Allyn & Bacon, 428–437.

Kulik, J.A., and C.L.C. Kulik. "Ability Grouping and Gifted Students." *Handbook of Gifted Education,* 1st ed., edited by N. Colangelo and G.A. Davis. Needham Heights, MA: Allyn & Bacon, 178–196.

Lerous, J.A. (1994). "A Tapestry of Values: Gifted Women Speak Out," *Gifted Education International* 9: 167–171.

Lind, Sharon. (Fall 2000). "Before Referring a Gifted Child for ADD, ADHD Evaluation," *California Gifted Association Communicator* 31 (4).

Lovecky, Deidre V. (1994). "Exceptionally Gifted Children: Different Minds," *Roeper Review* 17 (2): 16–20.

——. (1999). "Gifted Children with ADHD." Handout at the 11th Annual CHADD International Conference, Washington, DC.

Office of Educational Research and Improvement (1993). *National Excellence: A Case for Developing America's Talent.* Washington, DC: U.S. Department of Education.

Renzulli, Joseph S. (1978). "What Makes Giftedness? Reexamining a Definition," *Phi Delta Kappan* 60 (3): 180–84, 261.

Silverman, Linda. (1995). "To Be Gifted or Feminine," *The Journal of Secondary Gifted Education* 6: 141–153.

Smutny, Joan. (1999). "Gifted Girls," *Understanding Our Gifted* Winter: 9–13.

VanTassel-Baska, Joyce. (1991). "Serving the Disabled Gifted through Educational Collaboration," *Journal for the Education of the Gifted* 14, 246–266.

VanTassel-Baska, Joyce, and Bernadette Strykowski. (1988). *An Identification Resource Guide on the Gifted and Talented.* Evanston, IL: Northwestern University.

Chapter 3

Adderholdt, Miriam, and Jan Goldberg. (1999). *Perfectionism: What's Bad About Being Too Good?* Minneapolis: Free Spirit Publishing.

Bloom, Benjamin. (1985). *Developing Talent in Young People.* New York: Ballantine Books.

Delisle, Jim. (1987). *Gifted Kids Speak Out.* Minneapolis: Free Spirit Publishing.

Derevensky, Jeffrey, and Elaine B. Coleman. (1989). "Gifted Children's Fears," *Gifted Child Quarterly* 33 (2).

Gross, Miraca. (1993). *Exceptionally Gifted Children.* New York: Routledge.

Gross, M U M (1999). "Small Poppies: Highly Gifted Children in the Early Years," *Roeper Review* 21 (3): 207–214.

Hollingworth. L.S. (1942). *Children Above 180 IQ, Stanford-Binet: Origin and Development.* Yonkers, NY: World Book.

Kearney, K. (1992). "Life in the Asynchronous Family," *Understanding Our Gifted* 4(6), 1, 8–12.

Perry, Susan K. (2001). *Playing Smart: The Family Guide to Enriching, Offbeat Learning Activities for Ages 4–14.* Minneapolis: Free Spirit Publishing.

Rogers, Karen, and Linda K.Silverman. (1997). *A Study of 241 Extraordinarily Gifted Children.* National Association for Gifted Children 44th Annual Convention, Little Rock, AR.

Chapter 4

Ablard, K.E. (1997). "Self-perceptions and Needs as a Function of Type of Academic Ability and Gender," *Roeper Review* 20 (2): 110–115.

Adderholdt, Miriam, and Jan Goldberg. (1999). *Perfectionism: What's Bad About Being Too Good?* Minneapolis: Free Spirit Publishing.

Baker, J.A. (1995). "Depression and Suicidal Ideation Among Academically Talented Adolescents." *Gifted Child Quarterly* 39 (4): 218–223.

Bartell, N.P., and W.M. Reynolds. (1986). "Depression and Self-Esteem in Academically Gifted and Nongifted Children: A Comparison Study," *Journal of School Psychology* 24: 55–61.

Cornell, D. (1989). "Child Adjustment and Parent Use of the Term 'Gifted,'" *Gifted Child Quarterly* 33 (2): 59–64.

Cross, T.L. (1996). "Examining Claims About Gifted Children and Suicide," *Gifted Child Today* 19 (1): 46–48.

Dabrowski, K. (1964). *Positive Disintegration.* Boston: Little, Brown.

——. (1972). *Psychoneurosis Is Not an Illness.* London: Gryf.

Delisle, James. (1990). "The Gifted Adolescent at Risk: Strategies and Resources for Suicide Prevention Among Gifted Youth," *Journal for the Education of the Gifted* 13 (3), 212–228.

Dixon, D.N., and I.R. Scheckel. (1996). "Gifted Adolescent Suicide: The Empirical Base," *The Journal of Secondary Gifted Education,* 7 (3): 386–392.

Faber, Adele, and Elaine Mazlish. (1980). *How to Talk So Kids Will Listen, and Listen So Kids Will Talk.* New York: Avon.

Feldhusen, J., et al. (1990). "Self-Concepts of Gifted Children in Enrichment Programs," *Journal for the Education of the Gifted* 12: 380–387.

Garner, D. (1991). "Eating Disorders in the Gifted Adolescent," *Understanding the Gifted Adolescent.* Edited by M. Bierely and J. Genshaft. New York: Teachers College Press, 50–64.

Gordon, Thomas. (1989). *Teaching Children Self-Discipline at Home and at School.* New York: Random House.

Hewitt, P.L., G.L. Flett, and E. Ediger. (1996). "Perfectionism and Depression: Longitudinal Assessment of a Specific Vulnerability Hypothesis," *Journal of Abnormal Psychology* 105 (2): 276–280.

Hoge, R., and R. McSheffrey. (1991). "An Investigation of Self-Concept in Gifted Children," *Exceptional Children* 57: 238–245.

Howard-Hamilton, M., and B.A. Franks. (1995). "Gifted Adolescents: Psychological Behaviors, Values, and Developmental Implications," *Roeper Review* 17 (3): 186–191.

Jackson, P.S. (1998). "Bright Star—Black Sky: A Phenomenological Study of Depression as a Window into the Psyche of the Gifted Adolescent," *Roeper Review* 20 (3), 215–221.

Janos, P.M., H.C. Fung, and N. Robinson. (1985). "Self-Concept, Self-Esteem, and Peer Relations Among Gifted Children Who Feel 'Different,'" *Gifted Child Quarterly* 29: 78–81.

Janos, P.M., K.A. Marwood, and N. Robinson. (1985). "Friendship Patterns in Highly Intelligent Children," *Roeper Review* 8 (1): 46–49.

Johnson, Norine G., Michael Roberts and Judith Worell, eds. (2000). *Beyond Appearance: A New Look at Adolescent Girls.* Washington, DC: American Psychological Association.

Kerr, Barbara A., and Sanford J. Cohn. (2001). *Smart Boys: Talent, Manhood and the Search for Meaning.* Scottsdale, AZ: Great Potential Press, Inc.

Lind, Sharon. (2000). "Overexcitability and the Highly Gifted Child," *California Association for the Gifted Communicator* 31 (4).

McCallister, C., W.R. Nash, and E. Meckstroth. (1996). "The Social Competence of Gifted Children: Experiments and Experience," *Roeper Review* 18 (4): 273–276.

Neihart, M. (1991). Anxiety and Depression in High Ability and Average Ability Adolescents. *Dissertation Abstracts International.* (Doctoral dissertation: University of Northern Colorado).

Nelson, I. (1989). "Dabrowski's Theory of Positive Disintigration," *Advanced Development,* 1–14.

Panter, B., et al. (1995). *Creativity and Madness: Psychological Studies of Art and Artists.* Burbank, CA: American Institute of Medical Education.

Parker, W. (1996). "Psychological Adjustment in Mathematically Gifted Students," *Gifted Child Quarterly 40* (3): 154–157.

Parker, W., and Mills, C.J. (1996). "The Incidence of Perfectionism in Gifted Students," *Gifted Child Quarterly* 40 (4): 194–199.

Piechowski, Michael. (1991). "Emotional Development and Emotional Giftedness," *Handbook of Gifted Education,* 1st ed., edited by N. Colangelo and G.A. Davis. Needham Heights, MA: Allyn & Bacon, 285–306.

Roedell, W.C. (1984). "Vulnerabilities of Highly Gifted Children," *Roeper Review* 6: 127–130.

Roeper, Anne-Marie (1982). "How the Gifted Cope with Their Emotions," *Roeper Review* 5: 21–23.

Silverman, Linda K., ed. (1993). *Counseling the Gifted and Talented.* Denver, CO: Love Publishing.

Swiatek, M.A. (1995). "An Empirical Investigation of the Social Coping Strategies Used by Gifted Adolescents," *Gifted Child Quarterly* 39 (3): 154–161.

Tillier, W. (1999). *A Brief Overview of Dabrowski's Theory of Positive Disintegration and Its Relevance for the Gifted.* Available online at *members.shaw.ca/positivedisintegration.*

Tong, J., and L. Yewchuk. (1996). "Self-Concept and Sex-Role Orientation in Gifted High School Students," *Gifted Child Quarterly* 40 (1): 15–23.

Vaughn, V.L., J.F. Feldhusen, and J.W. Asher. (1991). "Meta-analyses and Review of Research on Pull-Out Programs in Gifted Education," *Gifted Child Quarterly* 35 (2): 92–98.

Webb, Jim, and D. Latimer. (1993). "ADHD and Children Who Are Gifted," *Exceptional Children* 60: 183–185.

Webb, Jim, Elizabeth Meckstroth, and Stephanie Tolan (1995). *Guiding the Gifted Child: A Practical Source for Parents and Teachers.* Scottsdale, AZ: Great Potential Press.

Chapter 5

Archambault, Francis X., et al. (1993). *Regular Classroom Practices with Gifted Students: Results of a National Survey of Classroom Teachers.* (Research Monograph No. 93102). Storrs, CT: The National Research Center on the Gifted and Talented (NRC/GT).

Bloom, Benjamin S., et al. (1984). *Taxonomy of Educational Objectives: Handbook of the Cognitive Domain.* New York, NY: Longman.

Burks, B.S., D.W. Jensen, and Louis Terman. (1930). *The Promise of Youth: Follow-up Studies of A Thousand Gifted Children,* vol. 3 of *Genetic Studies of Genius.* Stanford, CA: Stanford University Press.

Galbraith, Judy (1999). *The Gifted Kids' Survival Guide: For Ages 10 and Under.* Minneapolis: Free Spirit Publishing.

Galbraith, Judy, and James Delisle. (1996). *The Gifted Kids' Survival Guide: A Teen Handbook*. Minneapolis: Free Spirit Publishing.

Landrum, Mary, Carolyn Callahan, Beverly Shaklee, eds. (2001). *Aiming for Excellence: Annotations to the NAGC Pre-K–Grade 12 Gifted Program Standards*. Washington, DC: National Association for Gifted Children.

Morreale, Carol. (1993). "Rights of Students," Palatine, IL: Illinois Association for Gifted Children.

Office of Educational Research and Improvement. (1993). *National Excellence: A Case for Developing America's Talent*. Washington, DC: U.S. Department of Education.

Smutny, Joan F., Sally Walker, and Elizabeth Meckstroth. (1997). *Teaching Young Gifted Children in the Regular Classroom*. Minneapolis: Free Spirit Publishing.

Tomlinson, Carol Ann. (1999). *The Differentiated Classroom: Responding to the Needs of All Learners*. Alexandria, VA: Association for Supervision and Curriculum Development.

———. (1995). *How to Differentiate in the Mixed-Ability Classroom*. Alexandria, VA: Association for Supervision and Curriculum Development.

VanTassel-Baska, Joyce. (1988). *Comprehensive Curriculum for Gifted Learners*. Needham Heights, MA: Allyn & Bacon.

Winebrenner, Susan. (2001). *Teaching Gifted Kids in the Regular Classroom*. Minneapolis: Free Spirit Publishing.

Chapter 6

California Association for the Gifted (1998). *Advocacy in Action: An Advocacy Handbook for Gifted and Talented Education*. Whittier, CA: California Association for the Gifted.

Knopper, Dorothy. (1997). *Parent Education: Parents as Partners*. Boulder, CO: Open Space Communications.

———. (1989). "Profiles and Perspectives," *Roeper Review* 11 (4).

National Association for Gifted Children. (2000). *Advancing Gifted and Talented Education in Congress: An Advocacy Guide for Parents and Teachers*. Washington, DC: National Association for Gifted Children.

Smutny, Joan F. (2001). *Stand Up for Your Gifted Child*. Minneapolis: Free Spirit Publishing.

Stephens, K.R. (1998). "Promoting Gifted Education: A Parent's Guide to Public Relations." *Parenting for High Potential* 7: 15.

Council of State Directors of Programs for the Gifted. (1999). *The 1998–1999 State of the States Gifted and Talented Education Report*. Washington, DC: National Association for Gifted Children.

———. (2001). State of the States Gifted and Talented Education Report, 1999–2000. Washington, DC: National Association for Gifted Children.

Webb, J.T., and A. Devries. (1998). *Gifted Parent Groups: The SENG Model*. Scottsdale, AZ: Great Potential Press.

Index

About the Author

Dr. Sally Walker is the executive director of the Illinois Association for Gifted Children (IAGC) and works throughout the state to advocate for gifted children, their parents, and educators. Sally is the chair of the Gifted Advisory Council of Illinois and has written gifted language legislation for the state government. In 2007, the Illinois Association of Educational Office Professionals named her Illinois Administrator of the Year. Sally is also a consultant working in the field of gifted education, school improvement, and assessment. She has presented workshops and provided technical assistance to schools across the United States.

Sally has a doctorate degree in education, a master's degree in guidance and counseling and educational administration, and has completed postgraduate work in early childhood, gifted, and parent education. She is the coauthor of *Teaching Young Gifted Children in the Regular Classroom* (Free Spirit Publishing), *Acceleration for Gifted Learners, K–5* (Corwin Press), *Making Memories: A Parent Home Portfolio* (Pieces of Learning), and *A Guide for Parents: Overseeing Your Gifted Child's Education* (IAGC). She also has written numerous articles.

As a parent of three grown children, Sally testifies that if you can survive the frustrations and challenges of their childhood, kids can turn out to be wonderful, fascinating adults and your best friends.

Fast, Friendly, and Easy to Use

www.freespirit.com

Browse the catalog

Info & extras

Many ways to search

Quick check-out

Stop in and see!

Our Web site makes it easy to find the positive, reliable resources you need to empower teens and kids of all ages.

The Catalog.
Start browsing with just one click.

Beyond the Home Page.
Information and extras such as links and downloads.

The Search Box.
Find anything superfast.

Your Voice.
See testimonials from customers like you.

Request the Catalog.
Browse our catalog on paper, too!

The Nitty-Gritty.
Toll-free numbers, online ordering information, and more.

The 411.
News, reviews, awards, and special events.

 Our Web site is a secure commerce site. All of the personal information you enter at our site—including your name, address, and credit card number—is secure. So you can order with confidence when you order online from Free Spirit!

For a fast and easy way to receive our practical tips, helpful information, and special offers, send your email address to upbeatnews@freespirit.com. View a sample letter and our privacy policy at www.freespirit.com.

1.800.735.7323 • fax 612.337.5050 • help4kids@freespirit.com